# A Simple Guide
## to
# Birth Control

**Kamal K. Dutta, M.D., FACOG., FACS.**

NIPARI PUBLISHING
OAKLAND, NJ

Published by Nipari Publishing
www.birthcontroladvice.com

ISBN: 1-931991-50-2
Library of Congress Control Number: 2002103017

Printed in Canada
Book design: indypub, LLC
Cover Photo: Powerstock/Superstock


Publisher's Cataloging-in-Publication
*(Provided by Quality Books, Inc.)*

Dutta, Kamal K.
     A simple guide to birth control / Kamal K. Dutta. --
1st ed.
     p. cm.
     Includes bibilographical references and index.
     ISBN 1-931991-50-2

     1. Birth control--Popular works. 2. Contraception--
Popular works. I. Title.

RG136.2.D88 2002            613.9'4
                            QBI02-200236

# Dedications

*This book is dedicated to my parents:*
*who did their utmost to provide me with an excellent*
*education. They believed that education, especially*
*educating women throughout the world about their health,*
*results in a better life for everyone.*

*I would also like to dedicate this book to the reader:*
*for taking the necessary steps to take control*
*of their reproductive future and thus live a healthy,*
*responsible and self-determined life.*

*Also, to the physicians, nurses, researchers,*
*and others who devote their careers to developing*
*improved birth control options and informing*
*women of those choices.*

*Lastly, this book is dedicated to everyone who is fighting the*
*war on sexually transmitted diseases.*

# About the Author

Kamal Dutta, M.D., FACOG., FACS. is a board certified gynecologist with an active private practice and more than twenty years of experience in counseling women about their birth control choices. He is a Fellow of the American College of Obstetricians and Gynecologists and the American College of Surgeons and has served as Chairman of the Department of Obstetrics and Gynecology at two Passaic, New Jersey hospitals: General Hospital Center and St. Mary's Hospital. Dr. Dutta is also an Attending Gynecologist at Hackensack University Medical Center.

# Table of Contents

# Illustrations

# Preface

Even as we begin the new millennium, well ensconced in the "Information Age," a controversy remains concerning whether or not women, and their partners, have adequate knowledge about birth control choices. "Children having children" remains one of the greatest public health challenges of our generation.

Simply put, the purpose of birth control is to prevent unintended pregnancies. The ramifications of these pregnancies raise serious health concerns, not the least of which is the high rate of abortion throughout the world. Other consequences of unintended pregnancy include enormous economic costs, social stigma, and continuing a cycle of poverty. The fact remains that women who are least educated about birth control choices have more unplanned pregnancies. The statistics are alarming.

The 1995 National Survey of Family Growth Study indicates that 49% of all pregnancies were unintended, and 54% of these were terminated through elective abortion. The minority — 46% of unplanned pregnancies — resulted in birth. In 1994, there were about 5.38 million pregnancies in the United States (excluding 930,000 estimated miscarriages), approximately 3.95 million of which resulted in births and 1.43 million of which resulted in abortion. (It has been reported that 37% of married women and 65% of unmarried women who had unintended pregnancy sought abortion.)

There were 17.6 million women who visited their healthcare providers in 1995 seeking counsel or treatment relating to birth control. If you add visits due to sexually transmitted diseases (STDs), this number could be tripled or quadrupled. As the main focus of a physician's training is to take care of sick people, healthy young women often do not receive adequate attention from their healthcare provider on issues related to birth control. It takes time to counsel patients about the pros and cons of available methods, their costs, and the prevention of STDs. The inability of our healthcare system to educate women not only has grave public health consequences but also results in billions of dollars in unnecessary economic costs.

This book is intended to supplement the reader's knowledge and help the reader prevent unplanned pregnancies. It is intended for anyone who wants to prevent unintended pregnancy. This includes all women, married and unmarried, of childbearing age (usually between 15 to 45 years) and their partners. According to the National Survey of Family Growth, unintended pregnancies include pregnancies that occur:

A. Despite the use of birth control.

B. To women who don't want any or additional children.

C. To women who don't wish to be pregnant at that time, but may want to be later in life.

In addition to a lack of knowledge about their options, many women experience unplanned pregnancies because, for one reason or another, they were unable to afford the birth control method of their choice. The cost of birth control is very important to many patients, and this book is unique in that it provides practical ways to reduce the cost of contraception.

It is important to note that the main cost of birth control is neither the price of birth control methods nor the costs associated with treating the side effects. The birth control methods that are most cost-effective are those that are most reliable. Failure to prevent an unintended pregnancy places a financial burden on the couple and often on society as well. An entire chapter of this book is dedicated to discussing the effectiveness of different birth control methods. All reversible and irreversible methods are discussed, including new options introduced in 2002.

Also, misconceptions (by both teenagers and adults) about the correct use of methods and possible side effects contributes to many unplanned pregnancies. This book tries to dispel misconceptions for readers of all ages and help young people gain the knowledge they need to prevent unplanned pregnancies.

• • •

Birth control helps women plan their pregnancies — and plan their lives. Women who suffer from diabetes or high blood pressure should be especially encouraged to use proper birth control before getting pregnant. Preconception counseling helps many mothers-to-be plan their pregnancies for optimum outcome. For example, counselors can advise women to take folic acid supplements before getting pregnant to decrease the likelihood of their babies developing Spina Bifida. Women suffering from STDs such as HIV, Syphilis, Gonorrhea, Hepatitis and Chlamydia should get treated prior to getting pregnant to prevent transfer of the infection from the mother to the baby.

Birth control not only empowers women to make responsible choices regarding whether or not to become pregnant and bear a child, the proper spacing of children also has immense health benefits to mother and baby. Infants born within fifteen months after a sibling have a 33% greater chance of prematurity, low birth weight and serious health complications both during childbirth and later in life, when compared to children spaced further apart.

Currently, the media focuses on "children having children." It is well known that teenagers today are having sexual intercourse at an earlier age than in previous generations. The percentage of girls who have had sexual intercourse by age fiteen is 25%, by age sixteen the percentage is 40% and by age seventeen it is more than 50%. At the beginning of adult life, by age nineteen, more than 75% of teenagers have had sexual intercourse. Teenage girls are at the highest risk for complications associated with pregnancy and suffer the greatest economic disadvantages of any other age group faced with this responsibility.

• • •

It is impossible to address the health issues related to reproduction without educating women and their partners about sexually transmitted diseases. It is of life-and-death importance that anyone who is sexually active understands the health risks associated with sexual behavior, the protection offered - or lacking - in various birth control methods, and the potential health risks of STDs to unborn babies. Nearly 25% of Americans currently suffer from STDs or have suffered from them previously. There are more than twenty STDs known today, and they are spread by not practicing safe sex. The annual costs for treating STDs is about 10 to 15 billion dollars. Anyone wanting to avoid contracting or spreading STDs will find this book relevant as well.

• • •

In addition to traditional birth control methods, emergency birth control and its effectiveness are also discussed. Studies have shown that less than 20% of women have even heard of emergency birth control, an option that can effectively prevent many unintended pregnancies.

The purpose of this book is to make people aware about the importance of birth control in preventing unplanned pregnancies. We want women to take control of their reproductive lives, so they can better plan, improve the enjoyment of the lives and take better care of their health.

# Acknowledgments

I have not cited the innumerable sources and authorities that I consulted while writing this book. The list would include countless medical journals, libraries, institutions and many health professionals. I would like to thank the Center for Disease Control for its extensive work on birth control and sexually transmitted diseases (STDs).

I thank all of the people who made this book possible: My teachers, who taught me the real value of medical knowledge lies in sharing it with patients, to enable them to take better care of their own health, and the medical students and residents whose difficult questions helped me to better understand birth control and STDs.

I want to thank my family, Ruby, Tanya, Tia, and Sourav who made it all worthwhile.

But I am most grateful to my patients, who taught me by sharing their personal experiences about birth control. They inspired me to write this book and contributed by taking the time to discuss with me the advantages, disadvantages and costs of the different birth control methods they were using. Also, their personal pain in dealing with STDs proved to me the extreme importance of writing about the prevention of these diseases.

I hope this book will help many women better understand birth control and help them take more control over their reproductive life.

# Warning and Disclaimer

This book is meant to provide women with information that will help them better understand their birth control options. Neither the author nor the publisher are rendering medical advice to the reader. This book is not a substitute for a doctor and was not written as a comprehensive treatise on birth control, but rather as a simple, general guide. It is brief, in summary form and is for information purposes only. Readers are urged to learn as much as possible about birth control and discuss the options with their doctor to make the most informed choices. The contents of this book should not be used to make medical diagnoses or to choose treatments, nor should it be used as the reader's ultimate source of birth control advice. A physician's expertise, involvement and interaction with the reader is absolutely essential to making accurate medical diagnoses, prescribing treatments and recommending appropriate forms of birth control.

Readers are strongly advised against depending solely on the contents of this book or using the information contained in this book as reason to delay seeking professional medical advice and treatment. Physicians must see patients in person, review their medical records, complete a detailed medical history, perform a physical examination and have access to patients for follow-up medical care in order to recommend appropriate birth control methods. Readers should consult their doctor before making any birth control choices.

There are many differing and opposing views regarding the effectiveness, safety, side effects, benefits and all other aspects of every type of birth control method mentioned in this book. As this is a very dynamic field and constant research is going on to further our knowledge, the author and publisher make no guarantees or representation about the timeliness, completeness or reliability of the contents of this book. Readers are urged to review the package information supplied by the manufacturers of all medications and devices. Some of the birth control products mentioned in this book are patented products with registered trademarks belonging to specific companies.

The author and publisher shall have neither liability nor responsibility to any person or entity with respect to any loss or damaged caused, or alleged to have been caused, directly or indirectly, by the information contained in this book. The book may be returned to the publisher for a full refund, if the reader does not want to be bound by the disclaimer.

# Introduction

Almost all sexually active women of reproductive age have the possibility of getting pregnant. The time frame for pregnancy lasts about thirty years for most women. While the majority of women want children, most would prefer a planned pregnancy. Unfortunately, however, nearly half of all pregnancies are unplanned, and approximately 50% of those end in abortion.

Studies done on unintended pregnancy have shown that more than 65% of unmarried women who have unplanned pregnancies choose abortion. In the case of married women, the rate of abortion for unintended pregnancy is about 35% and rising. A possible reason for this is that with more women in the work force, families are more dependent on their earnings.

The main reason for using birth control is to prevent unintended pregnancies. When pregnancy is unplanned, statistics indicate a very high rate of abortion. Added to this is the increased health risks for mother and baby and the socioeconomic costs to the individual woman, her family and society at large. The United Nations "World Population Plan of Action" states, "all couples and individuals share the basic human right to decide freely and responsibly the number and spacing of their children, and to have the information, education and means to do so." *A Simple Guide to Birth Control* gives women the information they need to fully benefit from this right.

The main reasons for unplanned pregnancy are inadequate knowledge, low motivation to use birth control and the inconsistent and improper use of good and effective birth control methods. More than 50% of women who had an unplanned pregnancy were using some form of birth control method the year in which they got pregnant. The purpose of this book is to try to educate women of reproductive age about the importance of using proper birth control. This book is for all women of reproductive age—whether they are barely into their teens or well into their forties. The chance of getting pregnant for any woman within this age group is always present. Eighty percent of teenagers (eighteen and under) have had an unintended pregnancy, although the rate of abortion in this age group is decreasing. Some believe it is due to strong anti-abortion messages and convenient adoption services, while others believe it is due to decreased access to abortion services. The abortion rate for teenagers with an unintended pregnancy is about 45%, which is the lowest for any age group.

Conversely, for the age group between forty and forty-four, the unintended pregnancy rate is much greater than 50%, and the rate of abortion is 65% — the highest abortion rate for any age group.

For women between nineteen and forty years of age, the rate of unintended pregnancy is also very high, as is the rate of abortion. Nearly 50% of women in this age group have unplanned pregnancies, and approximately half of those pregnancies end in abortion. Poorer women have even a greater percentage of unintended pregnancies and higher corresponding abortion rates.

The consequences of unplanned pregnancies have been discussed at length by the media, but too little effort has been made to reduce the number of unintended pregnancies. This book is designed to help more women take control of their reproductive life. This is especially important for today's women who are more active, have careers and want to decide for themselves when, if and how many children they want to have. This guide dispels the myths of birth control and discusses the safety and effectiveness of the different methods. Emergency contraception, the special needs of teenagers and women over forty, the costs of different birth control methods and ways to reduce these costs are also explained. In addition, this book educates women about the symptoms, ramifications and prevention of sexually transmitted diseases.

# Part One
## *Overview*

# CHAPTER 1

## *The Importance of Birth Control*

With the recent increase in unplanned pregnancies and the tremendous rise in abortion rates, it is now more important than ever to educate women about birth control.

Did you know?

1. More than 50% of pregnancies in the United States are unintended, and more than half of such unintended pregnancies end in abortion.

2. Sexually transmitted diseases (STDs) are among the nations' most common, yet least understood, health problems. STDs affect approximately 15 million Americans every year — one-fourth of those infected are adolescents.

3. Some scientists estimate that one-fourth of the 2.3 million infertile couples in the U.S. are unable to conceive as a result of STD infections.

4. An estimated 43% of all US women in the US will have had an abortion by the age of 45.

Although the reasons for the high rate of both unplanned pregnancies and abortions are numerous, most of these pregnancies could have been prevented. The main reasons women face unplanned pregnancies are as follows:

- Many couples underestimate the woman's risk of pregnancy.

- Many couples do not use birth control, because they are overly concerned about the side effects.

- A serious lack of knowledge about the different methods of birth control and their effectiveness prevents many women from choosing a reliable and appropriate contraceptive. Women who are confused about their options may procrastinate about choosing a method and end up pregnant before they have had a chance to decide which form of birth control they should use.

- Many people use birth control incorrectly or inconsistently. Studies have shown that many women who have undergone abortion have at some point used a contraceptive.

It is crucial for people to understand how the different birth control methods work, and how they compare in terms of effectiveness, safety, side effects, protection against STDs and reversibility. By under-standing all of these factors, women and their partners are able to make informed decisions about birth control choices that take into account their personal needs and individual preferences.

Birth control methods can be divided into two major groups: reversible and irreversible. Reversible methods include birth control pills, hormones and intrauterine devices (IUDs). Irreversible methods include tubal ligation and vasectomy (female and male sterilization respectively).

The most reliable methods of reversible birth control are birth control pills, IUDs and hormones. Some hormones, such as Depoprovera and Lunelle, are administered by injection, while others, such as Norplant, are implanted under the skin. Reversible methods with higher failure rates include condoms, diaphragms and all other barrier methods.

Many people find it difficult to get all the information they need about birth control to enable them to fairly and thoroughly compare the different methods. As research advances doctors can give them updates on the latest contraceptive offerings, providing them with even more options. For example, although IUDs earned a very bad reputation years ago, because people associated them with causing infections of the uterus and fallopian tubes, the more modern IUDs cause minimal infection and can be a very good long-term birth control option.

Each patient should know her choices and be comfortable talking with her doctor about the best birth control for her stage of reproductive life. Methods of birth control used during adolescence are often inappropriate for women who have completed their family. Teenagers often rely on barrier methods to prevent pregnancies and STDs, but women in their twenties and thirties who want children usually seek a reversible method, such as birth control pills. After completing their family, they may choose tubal ligation or an IUD that can provide birth control for five to ten years. Finding a suitable birth control method can be one of the most significant factors in successfully shaping one's life.

# CHAPTER 2

## Advantages of
## Planned Pregnancies

There are several advantages in planning for pregnancies by using birth control. Many methods, apart from preventing pregnancy, have their own inherent health benefits. For example, birth control pills decrease the rate of some cancers and help prevent infection of the fallopian tubes. They also reduce breast cyst formation and decrease menstrual bleeding and cramps. The levonorgestrel Intrauterine Device (Mirena) decreases menstrual bleeding as well, and latex condoms are crucial in preventing sexually transmitted diseases (STDs).

Yet, the main purpose of birth control is to help women plan their pregnancies. This planning is especially important for women suffering from certain medical conditions, such as diabetes and high blood pressure. Pregnant women with diabetes that is under control are not in any increased risk of bearing children with congenital anomalies, but researchers have found that patients with uncontrolled diabetes are twice as likely to have babies with congenital problems. High blood pressure must be controlled prior to pregnancy, as it can cause severe complications for both the mother and baby. For instance, the baby could be stillborn, while the mother could have a severe hemorrhage, stroke or other serious medical complication if blood pressure is not properly controlled during pregnancy.

STDs should be diagnosed and treated prior to pregnancy. HIV, Syphilis, Gonorrhea, Chlamydia and Hepatitis can cause severe health problems for both the mother and baby. Although prenatal tests are routinely done for the above diseases, STDs should be controlled prior to pregnancy to prevent transmission of the disease from the mother to baby.

Another major benefit of planned pregnancy is that it gives women the ability to appropriately space their children. Studies have shown that babies born two years and three months to three years apart are healthier. Babies born within fifteen months of a previous birth are about one-third more likely to be born prematurely, which makes them more likely to be underweight and suffer from complications during both birth and later in life. (The type and severity of these complications depend on how extreme the prematurity is, which depends on the gestational age, size and weight of the baby at the time of delivery.)

Scientists believe that the reason it is so important to adequately space births is that a mother's body requires a certain amount of time to recover from pregnancy and childbirth. If a mother is breastfeeding, for instance, she is still sharing her nutrition with the newborn baby. If she gets pregnant during this time, her body could have difficulty coping with the increased physical and emotional stress.

Preconception counseling has become a very important tool for improving the timing and health of planned pregnancies. During pre-conception counseling the doctor advises patients to avoid toxic substances, such as alcohol and cigarettes. Alcohol used by the mother during conception and pregnancy can cause "Fetal Alcohol Syndrome." Smoking cigarettes not only increases the likelihood of miscarriages, but also is a major cause for low birth weight. There are also many drugs that should be avoided during conception and pregnancy. Many types of medications cause congenital abnormalities in fetuses. Also, it has been found that women who take supplemental folic acid prior to getting pregnant have a significantly lower chance of giving birth to babies with Spina Bifida. So, patients who are trying to conceive are advised to take vitamins containing 400 micrograms of folic acid per day.

There are nearly three deaths related to childbirth everyday in the United States. Throughout the world, the number of deaths related to childbirth is alarmingly high. The reasons for these deaths include severe bleeding, very high blood pressure (pre-ecclampsia and ecclampsia) and pulmonary embolism. These and other complications related to childbirth underscore the importance of avoiding unintended pregnancies. Other frequent complications include premature labor, miscarriage, severe vomiting, and infection. Researchers have found that one-third of women have complications during their pregnancy, and the cost of treating these complications is more than one billion dollars a year.

Black and Hispanic women are more likely to die from such complications than white women. Teenagers, unmarried women, those who have had no prenatal care, smokers and high school dropouts also have more complications during pregnancy. These women unfortunately also have increased rates of unintended pregnancy. In addition, women who have had one unintended pregnancy are more likely to have future unintended pregnancies.

There are multitude of advantages—and no disadvantages—for preventing unplanned pregnancy. In addition to helping ensure better health for women and their babies, the practice of carefully planning pregnancies can help women increase the success of their own lives and the health and well-being of their families.

# CHAPTER 3

## *Myths About Birth Control*

There are number of myths about birth control. It is important to discuss and dispel these misconceptions so that people will have the knowledge they need to evaluate and implement, with their doctor's guidance, the best method for their situation.

### Myth #1: *Birth control pills are dangerous.*

According to an American College of Gynecologists study, 75% of women incorrectly believe birth control pills are dangerous. Surveys have revealed that more than one-half of women believe that birth control pills pose a greater risk to their life than having a baby. This perception has persisted since the 1960s, when the pill initially came to the market. Thirty years ago birth control pills did contain a high dose of hormones with significant side effects. Yet, recent studies show that for a non-smoker under age thirty, the chance of death, while taking birth control pills, is less than one in 100,000. The chance of death from childbirth is estimated at eleven per 100,000 deliveries, or more than ten times the chance of death from birth control pills.

## Myth #2: *You don't get pregnant, if you douche immediately after sex.*

The sperm can move into the mouth of the cervix within thirty seconds. Douching only cleanses the vagina and does not prevent pregnancy.

## Myth #3: *Birth control pills should be stopped periodically.*

Reports have shown that one-half of women claiming to have some knowledge about birth control pills believe this myth. There is *no medical reason* to give the body "a break" from birth control pills. Using the pill intermittently does not bring change or decrease the side effects in any way. Women who want to stop taking the pill, even for a short time, should first discuss it with their doctor.

## Myth #4: *Women cannot get pregnant while breast-feeding.*

It is possible for women to become pregnant while breast-feeding. Although breast-feeding delays menstruation, ovulation can occur. For this reason, women who are breast-feeding should use some form of birth control.

### Myth #5: *Using birth control pills increase a woman's risk of getting cancer.*

More than 35% of women believe that the hormone in the pill increases the risk of cancer. However, there is no increased risk for breast cancer, and if a tumor does develop, it is usually detected at an earlier stage during one of the regular check-ups required of pill users. Moreover, birth control pills have been shown to reduce the risk of ovarian and uterine cancer.

### Myth #6: *Pills cause acne.*

Many teenagers believe that the pill causes or aggravates acne. On the contrary, studies show that birth control pills, especially the triphasic pills usually improve acne.

### Myth #7: *Pills cause weight gain.*

Many women, especially adolescents, choose not to use the pill, fearing an increase in their weight. Although some women do gain weight, others lose weight while taking birth control pills. Most women who take low-dose pills do not gain any weight at all, and 75% of those who do gain weight don't gain more than 3.5 pounds.

Very often, women on the pill gain weight for reasons unrelated to the birth control pills, but they attribute the weight gain to the pills. Women can usually solve this problem by eating a healthy diet and exercising regularly.

### Myth #8: *A man becomes impotent after a vasectomy.*

Vasectomy, a surgical procedure in which the spermatic cords are cut to prevent the passage of sperm from the testes to the penis, does not make men impotent. It merely prevents men from ejaculating sperm.

### Myth #9: *Women who use the rhythm method properly will not get pregnant.*

Although correct use of the rhythm method decreases the risk of pregnancy, it is possible for a woman to become pregnant while using this method. Many women believe that they can calculate the safe period during their cycles, but because the egg may be released at different times during irregular cycles, the safe period may be difficult to determine. Even women who have used the rhythm method successfully for long periods of time can end up pregnant after an irregular cycle.

**Myth #10:** *The most likely reason for a women to become pregnant when a condom has been used is condom breakage.*

The primary reason that women get pregnant or contract a sexually transmitted disease — even though their partner has used a condom — is that the condom was used incorrectly or inconsistently. The condom breakage rate is less that 2%, and every latex condom manufactured in the United States is tested for defects before it is packaged. This book describes in detail the steps to using condoms correctly to reduce the risk of pregnancy and disease.

**Myth #11:** *Sex education promotes sexual activity.*

Studies have shown that educating teens about sex and birth control does not lead to earlier or increased sexual activity in young people.

**Myth #12:** *Tubal ligation guarantees that a woman will not get pregnant.*

Even after undergoing a tubal ligation, it is possible for a woman to get pregnant, although the chances are less than 1%. If a woman who has had her tubes tied misses her period, she should take a pregnancy test as soon as possible. The chance of pregnancy in the fallopian tubes after tubal ligation is increased. It is extremely important to catch such a pregnancy early, since tubal ligation increases the risk of ectopic pregnancy, a potentially life-threatening condition that requires immediate surgery.

## Myth #13: *Withdrawal is a reliable method.*

The withdrawal method is very unreliable for two reasons. First of all, it requires the man to consistently and without fail withdraw his penis from the vagina prior to ejaculation. Secondly, because the penis usually leaks fluid that contains sperm before ejaculation, even successful withdrawal can result in pregnancy.

## Myth #14: *A woman who has had her tubes tied can easily have them untied, if she decides she wants more children.*

Many people believe that the term "tying the tubes" is a full and literal description of the tubal ligation procedure. Consequently, they think that if a woman who has undergone this procedure later decides that she wants to become pregnant, all she has to do is have her tubes untied. The reality is not that simple.

Tubal ligation usually involves tying, cutting and sometimes removing a segment of the fallopian tubes. The tubes may also be clamped or blocked with a device. When it is done through a laparoscope (a small telescope), the tubes are usually cauterized with electricity.

As a result, female sterilization is *not* easily reversible. Because sterilization is generally considered permanent, women considering it should be absolutely certain that they don't want more children. They should consider such scenarios as divorce or remarriage to test their conviction. Moreover, the decision should never be made immediately following a difficult pregnancy or an abortion.

# CHAPTER 4

## Birth Control
## for Teenagers

The group with the greatest need for knowledge about birth control is adolescent children. More and more teens are becoming sexually active at a younger age, with an increasing and alarming lack of knowledge about birth control. The percentage of girls who have had sexual intercourse by the age of fifteen is 25%. By age sixteen it's 40% and by seventeen it's more than 50%. By age nineteen, more than 75% of girls have had sex.

In 1996, the Alan Guttmacher Institute did a census study on pregnancies, revealing that in that particular year, there were 880,000 pregnancies among girls in the fifteen to nineteen-year-old group. Of these, 56% gave birth, 35% had an induced abortion, and 9% had a miscarriage or stillbirth.

Only 44% of adolescent women use some form of birth control in the first year they are sexually active. Of those who do use birth control, 40% take birth control pills, about 30% of their partners use condoms, 10% choose hormone injections, and 3% use Norplant to prevent pregnancy.

Among teenage girls, the failure rate with birth control pills is a startling 30%, compared with less than 2% for the general population. While some girls in this age group lack the maturity and the sense of responsibility to use birth control pills correctly, many simply don't understand the risks and consequences of their actions. These teenagers are not only highly likely to become pregnant, but also to contract sexually transmitted diseases (STDs).

In the US, teenagers account for more than a quarter of the 15 million people who contract STDs each year. The number of AIDS cases is also rising rapidly in those under twenty-five. Teenage girls show greater susceptibility to human papilloma virus, syphilis, chlamydia and gonorrhea because their vaginal tissue is weaker and more vulnerable to infection.

## Oral contraceptives for teenagers

Although few teenage girls realize it, birth control pills can be extremely beneficial in a variety of aspects. They prevent dysmenorrhea, a severe cramping of the uterus during menstruation, which can be incapacitating for some teenagers. Birth control pills help prevent the formation of ovarian cysts and some benign breast problems. Acne can also sometimes be thwarted through the use of birth control pills. In addition, pills reduce the chance of infection in the fallopian tubes by thickening the mucus at the mouth the womb, thereby preventing bacteria from moving inside. Birth control pills also regulate a woman's menstrual cycles to twenty-eight days, which is comforting to many young women with irregular cycles.

## Why do so many young women refuse to take birth control pills?

### Cost:

The cost of birth control pills is a concern for many young women. Although that cost may be covered under their parents' medical insurance, they are fearful, reluctant or unwilling to tell their parents.

### Side effects

Young women tend to worry a great deal about the side effects from taking birth control pills. There is a general misconception that pills are dangerous, so at the first sign of any side effect many young women discontinue their course of pills. Oftentimes, the grave concern about side effects has been passed down to young women from their mothers who used birth control pills years ago, when the amount of hormones in the pills was much higher and the side effects were sometimes severe.

- **Irregular bleeding:** For the first three to four months they are on the pill, some women have irregular bleeding, known as break-through bleeding. This is a common side effect for first-time pill users, but it can also happen if a woman does not take her pills at the same time each day. Usually, this bleeding gradually goes away on its own within four months. If it doesn't, the doctor can adjust the dosage.

- **Delayed periods:** Some women have scanty periods or completely miss a period while on the pill. Since the incidence of missed pills is very high for teenage girls a pregnancy test should be done as soon as possible following a missed period. If the problem persists, the dosage of the pills can be adjusted to take care of it, but the patient should not stop taking the pills on her own, without first discussing it with her doctor.

- **Breast cancer:** Many adolescents believe that there is a high probability of breast cancer while using the pill. All studies on the subject show, however, that there is no significant increase in breast cancer for women who take the pill. And because women on birth control pills undergo a check-up every six months, they benefit from early detection of breast cancer.

- **Weight gain:** It is a common misconception that birth control pills cause considerable weight gain, which is a serious concern to self-conscious teenagers. However, with low-dose oral contraceptive pills, there is very little chance of weight gain. In fact, studies have shown that adolescents who take triphasic pills(see page 74 under "The Combination Pill") have the same rate of weight gain as adolescents who don't take any birth control pills. The low-dose pill also causes less bloating, but most young women consider any bloating unacceptable if it gives the appearance of weight gain. If weight gain or bloating are a persistent problem, the type of pill and/or dosage can be changed.

- **Acne:** Another widely spread misconception is that birth control pills cause or worsen acne. In reality most birth control pills do not contribute to acne. In fact, they often improve it. Triphasic pills in particular have been proven to improve acne. However, if acne remains a problem, the doctor can change the pill and/or adjust the dosage.

The other common reasons that teenage girls have for discontinuing the pill are nausea, breast tenderness and headaches. Although many of these side effects disappear within three months, it is important for women to bring all side effects to the attention of their doctor.

*(Please read the chapter on birth control pills to learn how to use birth control pills correctly.)*

## Condoms for Teenagers

Although birth control pills are the most popular birth control choice among teenagers, condoms should always be used additionally to prevent STDs. In order to be effective, condoms must be used correctly *every time* there is sexual contact.

## Other Birth Control Methods

All of the birth control methods mentioned below should be used with a condom to protect not only against pregnancy, but also against STDs.

- Intrauterine device: This is rarely used by adolescents, except those who already have children.

- Depoprovera injection: About 10% of adolescents who use birth control receive Depoprovera injections.

- Norplant implants: 3% of teenagers who use birth control rely on Norplants.

- Diaphragm: This method is rarely appropriate for teenagers, as it requires discipline and forethought to use correctly.

- Natural family planning method: Teenagers should be aware that these methods have a much higher rate of pregnancy than all of the other previously mentioned methods.

## Emergency Birth Control

Emergency birth control is an important option for many women, including adolescents. Studies show that women who are less than twenty-five years old and who do not have children are most likely to use emergency birth control. Please read the chapter on emergency birth control to learn when this method is appropriate. Emergency birth control should *never* be used as the sole method of contraception, but only as a backup.

# CHAPTER 5

## Birth Control Above Age Forty

Women over the age of forty face a unique challenge in choosing, and using, the proper birth control method. While the chance of pregnancy decreases after age forty (the average age of menopause is approximately fifty), there are still many women who become pregnant in their forties.

Unfortunately, many women mistakenly believe that since they are above forty years old they cannot get pregnant. This is simply not true.

It is true that women in their forties are more likely to have delayed periods. Also, the fear of having an unintended pregnancy may be quite intense, because most older women have completed their family and do not want any more children. Age is a big factor in the concern women over forty may feel about the increased risk to their own health and their unborn baby's health.

If women over forty do become pregnant, more than 65% will choose to have an abortion. This rate of abortion is higher than any other age group including teens.

## Birth Control Pills

Today, most doctors agree that birth control pills can be used safely until age forty-five for women who do not have any risk factors for birth control usage. For women who smoke more than fifteen cigarettes a day, birth control pills are usually not advised after age thirty-five. Since many pills nowadays are low-dose pills, many women continue using the pills until they reach menopause, after which they use hormone replacement therapy (HRT).

Birth control pills have many advantages and some disadvantages. One of the many advantages of the pill is better control of the menstrual period. Another is that women are likely to have more regular check-ups when on birth control pills. There is also less risk of ovarian cysts, fibrocystic breast disease as well as pelvic infections. The pills also decrease the incidence of cancer of the ovaries and cancer of the uterus. (For further information, please read the chapter on "Birth Control Pills").

## Intrauterine Device

An Intrauterine Device (IUD) is a very good option for this age group. The Paraguard can be used for a long time and is economical. Also, it is effective immediately, and the chance of pregnancy is less than 1%. Mirena can also be used, and it is also cost affective, as it does not have to be replaced for five years.

## Condoms and Diaphragms

Women above forty have less failure rates with the barrier methods such as condoms and diaphragms than other age groups. The reason for this is that they and their partners are more mature and use these contraceptives correctly and consistently. The condoms have an added advantage of preventing sexually transmitted diseases. This is an individual issue, as women in this age group usually have a more stable, monogamous relationship than other age groups.

## Norplant

Norplant can be used in women above age forty. This is a good long-term contraceptive with the only disadvantage being that minor surgery is required to insert the capsules and also to remove it.

## Depoprovera

This is a very good contraceptive. The advantages are that it has to be taken once every three months and it is very effective. The main side effective is absence of period and delayed fertility. In the above age group these two factors are not considered disadvantages.

## Natural Family Planning

Many women, due to personal reasons, want to use natural family planning methods. This includes the Basal Body Temperature, Cervical Mucus and Rhythm Method. Although these methods are not advisable in the younger age group, women above 40 can use them with decreased failure rates. The reason is that these women and their partners are much more mature and they are more apt to use these methods correctly.

## Sterilization

Female sterilization (tubal ligation) is the most commonly used form of birth control in this age group. Vasectomy means male sterilization and is less complicated, less painful and easier to perform than female sterilization. Many women prefer sterilization, as they do not have to worry about birth control anymore. Studies have shown that female sterilization does not increase menstrual irregularity as many women commonly think.

Having the right birth control choice is very important in this age group, as women are more afraid of an unplanned pregnancy than any other age group. Taking control of their reproductive life is very important and the right choice can enrich their sexual life.

## Sexually Transmitted Diseases in Women above Age Forty

Many women above age forty are at high risk for contracting sexually transmitted diseases. As more women think that they do not have any need for birth control, they forget that they can get sexually transmitted diseases. Data presented by the American College of Gynecologists showed that elderly women may be at a high risk, because they might be recently separated or divorced from their husbands and may have multiple sexual partners. Many women in this age group have herpes or are infected with Human Papilloma Virus. *(Please read the chapter on "Sexually Transmitted Diseases" and "Prevention of Sexually Transmitted Diseases.")*

# CHAPTER 6

## *Effectiveness of Various Birth Control Methods*

One of the most important concerns with birth control methods is their effectiveness. Women should also be aware of which methods are reversible and which are irreversible. Reversible methods can be stopped when the woman wants, allowing her to get pregnant. With irreversible methods, fertility cannot be restored unless major surgery is done to open the blocked tubes.

Statistical data indicates that the average age a woman first has intercourse is about seventeen and one-half years. The average age for menopause is about fifty years. The average age of a woman when she has her first baby is around twenty-four years, and she is usually done childbearing by age thirty. Keep in mind that these are averages. Actual individual ages for these events vary widely.

Women generally need contraception for some *thirty years* of their lives. Birth control is important not only to avoid unwanted pregnancies, but also to appropriately space the birth of their children.

Before women are married, they usually want a reliable, reversible form of long-term contraception. For the first few years of marriage, women often want a shorter-term, reversible form of contraception. When they have completed their family, they usually want a long-term birth control method.

The reliable methods of reversible birth control are birth control pills, Depoprovera, Norplant and intrauterine devices. The rate of pregnancy is measured in terms of the percentage of women who will get pregnant in a year using a particular form of birth control. For instance, if the rate of pregnancy for a method is one percent, that means that one out of one hundred women will get pregnant within a year, while using that method in the exact manner in which it was advised. Doctors refer to this as the "lowest expected pregnancy rate." The "typical rate" is the rate of pregnancy for the general population and it assumes that the method is not used exactly as advised. There is some variation in these numbers, depending on the type of pill or IUD used. The following are the typical pregnancy rates for the reliable methods of reversible birth control:

- Intrauterine Device — less than 1%
- Norplant — less than 1%
- Depoprovera — less than 1%
- Combination Pill — less than 2%
- Mini Pill (Progestin) — less than 3%
- Contraceptive Skin Patch — less than 1%

Reliable methods of irreversible birth control are tubal sterilization and vasectomy. The chance of pregnancy after these procedures is less than 1%. Although tubal sterilization and vasectomy are generally considered irreversible, in some cases the tubes can be successfully unblocked and put back together. These are complicated operations, and the chance of success is not great. Therefore, women should be sure that they do not want any future children before opting for sterilization.

Less reliable methods of reversible birth control include condoms, diaphragms, cervical caps, spermicides, withdrawal and fertility awareness methods. Fertility awareness methods include rhythm method, basal body temperature method and cervical mucus method. The typical pregnancy rates (percentages are approximate) for these methods are given below:

- 85%: No method
- 15%: Condoms without spermicide*

# EFFECTIVENESS OF VARIOUS METHODS

- 10%: Condoms with spermicides
- 20%: Female condom
- 20%: Diaphragm
- 20%: Cervical cap
- 20%: Spermicide alone
- 25%: Withdrawal
- 20%: Basal body temperature method
- 20%: Rhythm method
- 20%: Cervical mucus method

*\* Spermicides include spermicidal jelly, foam, gel, tablets and suppositories.*

# CHAPTER 7

## Reducing the Cost of Birth Control

The cost of the birth control is a real concern for many women. In many cases, health insurance coverage determines the type of birth control a woman will use.

The 1995 National Survey of Family Growth Study revealed that 28% of women rely on female sterilization, 27% use birth control pills, 3% use Depoprovera or Norplant, 2% use a diaphragm, and less than 1% use an intrauterine device (IUD). Condoms and vasectomy are used by 20% and 11% of men respectively.

According to the American College of Gynecologists, although the pill is often used for its non-contraceptive benefits, many insurance companies still will not cover it. This discourages many women from using it. The high rate of female sterilization is a response both to the expense of other reliable birth control methods and the reluctance of women in the US to even consider the IUD as a viable option. This is truly a loss for many women. The IUD is as effective as tubal ligation and vasectomy, does not require surgery and is one of the least expensive long-term methods of birth control. Plus, unlike sterilization, it can be reversed easily. (After the IUD string is pulled out, the woman becomes fertile again.) Yet, most women won't consider the IUD, and many doctors won't insert it. This resistance stems from problems of pelvic infection with the Dalkon Shield, a type of IUD that was on the market a number of years ago. Although the new IUDs are much safer, the stigma persists.

In Europe, more than 25% of women use the IUD as the birth control method, and throughout the world it is the most commonly used birth control method. If the IUD can make a comeback in the U.S., then the cost of birth control will be reduced greatly for many women.

The cost of birth control includes:

- The price of the pills, device, or procedure.
- The cost of treating the side effects of the method.
- The cost of unplanned pregnancies.

Most researchers believe that the price of a birth control method and the cost of its side effects determines only a small portion of its overall cost-effectiveness. Rather, the cost-effectiveness is more dependent on the ability of the method to successfully prevent unplanned pregnancies. Studies have shown that over a five-year period, the female condom and cervical cap are most costly, due to their high rate of failure. The least costly birth control method is the Copper T IUD, followed by vasectomy, Norplant implants and Depoprovera injections. In addition to these, other reliable methods of birth control that are less costly over a long period of time, include the Progesterone T IUD, Mirena (Levonorgestrel IUD), Lunelle (monthly contraceptive injection), birth control pills, and tubal ligation.

Although male condoms are one of the more costly methods, because the chance of pregnancy is relatively high, its use is extremely important to prevent sexually transmitted diseases.

Other "costly" contraceptives with a relatively high failure rate include spermicides and diaphragms. Even periodic abstinence and withdrawal, which don't cost anything to use and have no side effects, are considered costly when used over a long period of time, because of their high risk of pregnancy. So, how do you reduce the cost? Start by discussing with your doctor all the advantages, disadvantages, and costs involved for the birth control method(s) you are currently using. But, remember that cost should not be the only factor you consider.

As mentioned earlier, IUDs are cheaper long term than all other reliable forms of birth control. The Paraguard IUD, for example, costs approximately about $600 for the IUD and insertion. However, if the IUD is used for ten years, the monthly cost is about $5.

The cost of brand birth control pills is high, and pills must be taken consistently in order to effectively prevent pregnancy. Many insurance companies do not cover birth control pills, and the high cost sometimes prevent women from using birth control pills every month. However, generic equivalents of brand products are usually just as effective and safe and cost much less. Many women have been transferred from brand to generic birth control pills, because most HMOs only cover generics. These patients usually do well on generic pills. Although, you can get information about generic equivalents from your pharmacist, you should not change your birth control pill without first discussing it with your doctor.

The reason for the low cost of generics is that the manufacturer does not have to pay for research and advertising. The drug company develops a pill, can hold exclusive rights to the patent for many years, during which only that company can sell the pill as a brand product. After the patent expires, other companies are allowed to make a generic "unbranded" version and sell it cheaper.

On the opposite page is a list that contains the approximate price of some brands and their generic equivalents. For patients insured by HMOs, if you want a particular brand of birth control, you may have to pay a larger co-pay. If you switch to a generic birth control pill, the co-pay may be much less or non-existent. But remember, cost should not be the only factor you consider.

As far as the other methods of birth control, call around to local pharmacies and drug stores to get the best price. There can be a significant difference from one store to another in the prices of condoms, spermicides, IUDs and Depoprovera. You can also save money by buying your birth control by mail order. Sometimes, if you order three months of birth control pills at one time, you can get a cheaper rate. Don't be afraid to shop around, and don't feel shy about discussing with your doctor how you can reduce the cost of birth control.

| Brand Drug & Cost | | Generic Drug & Cost | | Difference Per Month | Difference Per Year |
|---|---|---|---|---|---|
| Ortho-Novum (1/35)-28 | $31.45 | Genora (1/35)-28 | $ 8.58 | $22.87 | $274.44 |
| Ortho-Novum (1/50)-28 | $31.45 | Genora (1/50)-28 | $ 9.25 | $22.20 | $266.40 |
| Ortho-Novum (10/11)-28 | $34.31 | Nelova (10/11)-28 | $15.05 | $19.26 | $231.12 |
| Ortho-Cept | $31.45 | Apri | $23.64 | $ 7.81 | $ 93.72 |
| Nordette-21 | $31.93 | Levora-21 | $28.51 | $ 3.42 | $ 41.04 |
| Nordette-28 | $31.93 | Levora-28 | $26.61 | $ 5.32 | $ 63.84 |
| Lo/Ovral-21 | $32.72 | Low-Ogestrel-21 | $28.01 | $ 4.71 | $ 56.52 |
| Lo/Ovral-28 | $32.73 | Low-Ogestral-28 | $29.35 | $ 3.38 | $ 40.56 |
| Modicon | $34.31 | Necon-21 | $30.76 | $ 3.55 | $ 42.60 |
| Ovral-28 | $50.10 | Ogestrel-28 | $44.92 | $ 5.18 | $ 62.16 |
| Demulen (1/35)-21 | $31.39 | Zovia (1/35)-21 | $28.43 | $ 2.96 | $ 35.52 |
| Demulen (1/35)-28 | $33.31 | Zovia (1/35)-28 | $28.72 | $ 4.59 | $ 55.08 |
| Demulen (1/50)-21 | $35.02 | Zovia (1/50)-21 | $31.70 | $ 3.32 | $ 39.84 |
| Demulen (1/50)-28 | $35.36 | Zovia (1/50)-28 | $32.00 | $ 3.36 | $ 40.32 |
| Triphasil-28 | $30.54 | Trivora-28 | $26.43 | $ 4.11 | $ 49.32 |

# CHAPTER 8

## Emergency
## Birth Control

### What is emergency birth control?

Emergency oral contraceptive, also known as the "morning after pill" or "postcoital contraceptive" is a method to prevent pregnancy following unprotected vaginal intercourse. This chapter deals with questions patients commonly ask when they are prescribed emergency oral contraception.

### Who should be prescribed emergency contraception?

Any woman who is at risk of becoming pregnant and who has had unprotected sexual intercourse up to seventy-two hours prior to treatment may be prescribed such contraception. Use of emergency contraception is not linked with the timing of sex in the menstrual cycle.

Studies have shown that the women seeking emergency birth control are usually less than twenty-five years old and do not have children.

Two of the most common reasons for using this type of contraception are the lack of any birth control during a sexual act and condom breakage. Other reasons include miscalculation of the "safe days" by the woman and unsuccessful withdrawal by her partner prior to ejaculation. Many women use emergency birth control as a backup method when they doubt the adequacy of the form of contraception they have been using. Such doubts occur when women miss their birth control pills, or when a diaphragm or female condom has been inserted incorrectly, leaving the woman at risk of becoming pregnant.

## What are the methods of emergency contraception?

The initial emergency contraception method was known as the Yuzpe method. It consisted of two tablets—each of ethinyl estradiol and dl-norgestrel, 0.5mg, taken twelve hours apart. The woman being treated with this method took a total of four tablets. There are many birth control pills that, when taken in combination, can provide the same results as the Yuzpe method. At present, two products have FDA approval as emergency contraceptives. Preven (Gynetics, Bele Mead, N J) consists of four tablets, each containing 0.05 mg ethinyl estradiol and 0.25 mg levonorgestrel. The second FDA-approved product, Plan B (Women's Capital Corp., Bellevue Wash.), was released more recently and contains two tablets each of which contain, 0.75 mg of levonorgestrel.

## Effectiveness of emergency contraception

The effectiveness of this type of treatment is 75%. Patients must understand that the 75% rate of effectiveness does not automatically imply a 25% chance of pregnancy. For instance, if one hundred women have unprotected intercourse in the middle two weeks of their cycle, which is from the seven to the twenty-first day (the first day of the cycle is the first day of the period), ordinarily only about eight will become pregnant. After using emergency birth control, that number is reduced to two. Emergency birth control should never be used as a substitute for the consistent use of other birth control methods. As stated in the name, it should be only used in cases of emergency.

## How does emergency contraception work?

Most scientists believe that it changes the uterine lining, thus preventing implantation. Others believe that it prevents ovulation or interferes with fertilization by trapping the sperm in thick cervical mucus. But once implantation has taken place, emergency birth control will not work.

## When does a woman start the treatment?

Usually the best time to take emergency contraception tablets is right after active intercourse. Many scientists believe that the effectiveness is still retained if it is taken at any time in the first seventy-two hours after intercourse. Most doctors feel that the earlier the tablets are taken, the better the chance of preventing pregnancy. So, the best advice to women is to take the tablets as soon as possible following intercourse.

## Side effects

- Nausea and vomiting are noted as the main side effects of emergency oral contraceptive. Nausea occurs in 50% of patients and vomiting occurs in 20%. The incidents of nausea and vomiting can be reduced, if antiemetics (medication to prevent nausea and vomiting) are taken one hour before the emergency pills are administered.

- Another potential side effect is breast tenderness.

  *Some doctors believe that Plan B, the newer of the two products, has fewer side effects.*

## How does emergency birth control effect the next period?

Nearly 98% of women will menstruate within twenty days of the treatment, and 90% of patients usually have normal periods. The average time until the next period is eight days. The onset of the period may be delayed, if the pills were taken in the second half of the woman's menstrual cycle. It is advisable to inform the doctor if menstruation does not occur within twenty-one days.

## What happens to the baby, if the patient gets pregnant after having used emergency birth control?

As there is no increased risk of birth defects after using monthly oral contraceptives, it is highly unlikely that the baby will suffer any consequences after the use of only a few pills for this emergency method.

## Getting a prescription for emergency birth control

If you think there is a possibility that you might need an emergency contraceptive in the future, you can request that your physician give you a prescription during a routine visit. A physician who has not seen you might be wary about giving you such a prescription. So, before you get into a situation where you might need emergency birth control, you should make sure that the doctor will be available to prescribe the medication immediately. In many countries, including Norway, France, and England, the emergency birth control pill is sold over the counter.

## Who should not use emergency birth control?

Most doctors agree that women can use emergency birth control, even if they were not appropriate candidates for other types of birth control pills. It is important for women to discuss with the doctor any other medical problems that might contraindicate the use of emergency birth control pills.

## Costs

- The cost will be $24 to $28

## IUD as Emergency Birth Control

In rare situations a doctor inserts an IUD after a woman has unprotected sex. This insertion is done within seven days. This is only done if the woman wants a long term contraceptive. It is thought that the IUD prevents implantation and thereby stops the pregnancy.

## 1-888-NOT-2-LATE

If you are unable to find a doctor or clinic that will provide emergency contraception, you can call 1-888-NOT-2-LATE. They will provide the names of about three to five practitioners in your surrounding area who can prescribe emergency birth control.

# Part Two
*Reversible Methods*

# CHAPTER 9

## Birth Control Pills

This chapter discusses the various types of birth control pills and their side effects.

## What is the pill?

The birth control pill, or "the pill" as it is widely known, is an oral contraceptive and one of the most effective, popular and reliable means of preventing pregnancy. Pills are reversible method of birth control, which means that a woman can become pregnant again after she stops taking the pills.

The patient should always discuss with her healthcare provider in detail about oral contraceptives including their side effects before beginning any course of pills.

IT IS EXTREMELY IMPORTANT TO REMEMBER, HOWEVER, THAT THE PILL DOES NOT OFFER ANY PROTECTION AGAINST SEXUALLY TRANSMITTED DISEASES, INCLUDING HIV.

## How does the pill work?

Birth control pills taken regularly, as prescribed, work by using hormones to prevent the release of the egg from the ovary This eliminates the possibility of pregnancy. Combination pills also help to thicken the cervical mucus to prevent the sperm from entering the cavity of the uterus. The "Progestin only pill" also thickens the mucus in addition to preventing the release of the egg.

The menstrual cycle is controlled by hormones, progesterone and estrogen. These chemical messengers are ruled by the brain to send signals to the ovary to release the egg. Birth control pills are made up of synthetic hormones called progestin and estrogen, which mimic the body's natural sex hormones to stop the egg from being released.

## Types of birth control pills

Birth control pills are divided into two basic types, depending on which hormone they contain.

# How the Pills Work

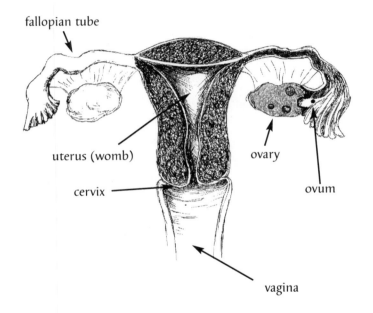

fallopian tube

uterus (womb)

cervix

ovary

ovum

vagina

Note: The fallopian tube and ovary on the right side of the drawing are shown as a cross-section, to reveal the ovum (egg) coming out of the ovary and into the fallopian tube.

## The Combination Pill

This type of pill contains both estrogen and progestin, which is why it is called the combination pill. The combination pill is divided into three types: monophasic, biphasic, and triphasic.

1. Monophasic birth control pills deliver the same dose of estrogen and progestin throughout the month.

2. Biphasic and triphasic pills deliver varying amounts of progestin and estrogen throughout the menstrual cycle, so the amount of hormones the body receives in the beginning of the cycle is different from the amount it receives at the end of the cycle. Active hormones are only present in the first twenty-one tablets.

3. Triphasic pills are currently the most common type of birth control pills. During a natural menstrual cycle, the amount of sex hormones produced by the body varies throughout different phases of the cycle. The triphasic pill tries to follow this natural fluctuation of the hormones. These pills deliver only the necessary amount of hormones to ensure effectiveness. Such low dose of hormones reduce the number and severity of side effects for many women.

## "Progestin-Only" Pill

Commonly known as "the mini pill" and "POP," "progestin only" pills provide a constant dose of progestin, but the amount is lower than the dose of progestin found in combination pills. Also, in contrast to combination pills, which have twenty-one tablets of active hormones and seven days of "reminder pills" the progestin only pills consist of twenty-eight tablets of active hormones. Progestin-only pills are used by women who cannot take estrogen, including mothers who are breastfeeding.

## What is the low-dose pill?

The dose of synthetic sex hormones in birth control pills has declined significantly since the pill was first introduced to the market in the 1960s. At that time, the pill caused many side effects. Because the sole purpose of the pill in the 1960s was preventing pregnancy, very little attention was paid to its side effects. Later, it was discovered that pregnancy could be prevented using much lower dosages of hormones and, consequently, with fewer side effects.

Oral contraceptives are considered "high dose" if they contain more than 50 micrograms of estrogen; "moderate dose" if they contained 50 micrograms of estrogen; and "low dose" if they have less than 50 micrograms. Currently, there are low dose pills that have as little as 20 micrograms of estrogen.

Because the knowledge about hormones is changing rapidly, in the future birth control pills may contain even less hormones and provide even greater effectiveness in pregnancy prevention with fewer side effects.

## The cost of the pill

- The cost of a physical examination by a doctor can range from $60 to $150, and the cost of the pill usually ranges from $20 to $40.
  *(To learn how to get birth control pills at a reduced price, read the chapter on "Reducing the Cost of Birth Control.")*

## Benefits of the pill

The pills offer many health benefits. Apart from preventing pregnancy, the pill does not interfere in the act of intercourse in any way. Also, since the chance of getting pregnant with the pill is greatly reduced, a woman does not have to worry about getting pregnant, which enhances her sex life.

- **Changes in the menstrual cycle.:** After starting birth control pills, women usually experience monthly periods that are more regular, lighter and less painful.

- **Prevention of acne:** Studies have revealed that the pill, especially the triphasic pill, reduces acne.

- **Prevention of cancer:** The pill helps prevent cancer of the ovaries and cancer of the lining of the womb.

- **Less risk of ovarian cysts:** The pill helps reduce the occurrence of ovarian cysts, which are fluid-filled growths that sometimes form on the ovary during ovulation. A common condition among women, ovarian cysts can enlarge, causing severe pain, and even rupture. In some cases, surgery is necessary to remove the cyst.

- **Less risk of fibrocystic breast disease:** Birth control pills reduce the risk of fibrocystic breast disease, a condition where the milk-producing glands thicken and feel like breast lumps.

- **Reduced risk of pelvic inflammatory disease:** Infection of the fallopian tubes, also known as pelvic inflammatory disease (PID), is a serious bacterial infection that, in severe cases, can result in infertility. The pill thickens the cervical mucus at the mouth of the womb, creating a barrier to prevent bacteria from entering the cavity of the womb and thereby reducing the risk of PID. In addition, women who use birth control pills have a lower chance of ectopic pregnancy (a pregnancy that occurs in the fallopian tubes), because the pill prevents the ovaries from releasing eggs.

## Women who should not take the pill

Although the pill is generally considered one of the safest forms of birth control, some women should not use it for medical reasons. They include those with:

- undiagnosed abnormal vaginal bleeding,
- known or suspected cancer of the lining of the womb,
- known or suspected cancer of the breast or an abnormal growth on the breast,
- inflammation of the veins or incidence of blood clots,
- tumors of the liver,
- known or suspected pregnancy,
- jaundice,
- very high cholesterol levels,
- high blood pressure, or
- complications of diabetes mellitus.

## Relative contra-indications to oral contraceptive use

Women with the following risk factors should use birth control with extreme caution:

- diabetes,
- those who take other drugs or medications that can interact badly with birth control pills,
- migraine or other kinds of vascular headache,
- smoking, for women above the age of thirty-five, or
- slightly high cholesterol or slightly elevated blood pressure.

Some doctors believe that the pill should not be prescribed at all to women who smoke after the age of thirty-five. Even women younger than thirty-five who smoke should be advised to quit, especially if they take the pill. Women should read the patient package insert and detailed patient labeling carefully to understand all the risks and contra-indications before taking any birth control pill.

## Side effects of the pill

Women should inform their doctor of any abnormal

symptoms they experience while on the pill. The reason the pill is available only with a prescription is because a doctor's supervision is necessary.

Some side effects of the pill may disappear within the first four months. If a woman understands this before starting the pill, she is likely to have a much higher success rate at taking the pill long term. In addition, it is important that women understand how to deal with the common side effects of the pills.

- Menstrual irregularity: The most common reason that women stop taking the pill is that they feel uncomfortable with the menstrual changes it causes. About 25% of women on the pill experience irregular spotting or bleeding, though for most women it ceases entirely within the first four months.

- Amenorrhea (absence of menstrual period) It is possible for a woman to skip her period entirely while on the pill. If this happens, the woman should take a pregnancy test, even though her chance of pregnancy is less than 2% if she is taking the pill properly. She should also tell her doctor, who can prescribe a different low dose combination pill to keep her menstrual cycle regular.

## Other Side Effects

Other side effects that can result from taking the pill include:

- headaches
- nausea, and
- breast tenderness.

  *(Although these symptoms often disappear on their own within four months, patients should alert their doctor of any problems they are having. In some cases, switching to another type of birth control pill easily solves the problem.)*

- breast cancer and birth control pills: Most studies on women aged twenty to fifty-four who have used the pills in the past have shown that they experienced no increase of breast cancer. Research has also shown that pill users with a history of benign breast diseases experienced no increased risk from the pill. Moreover, women with a family history of breast cancer and those who have used birth control pills for a very long time show no increased risk of breast cancer.

- weight gain and birth control pills: Concern over weight gain is one of the main reasons that women discontinue the pill.

Studies were conducted on two groups of women: one using triphasic pills and the other using no pills. The comparative study showed very little difference in weight gain among the two groups of women. However, many women perceive bloating as weight gain, even though it is part of their natural hormonal cycle. If women eat a healthy diet and exercise, the feeling of bloating and heaviness may disappear entirely.

## When should you report to your doctor?

Women on the pill should contact the doctor immediately if any of the following symptoms develop:

- unexplained body pain,
- pain, redness or swelling of the legs,
- blurred vision,
- yellowing of the skin, or
- severe headaches.

*If a woman wants to discontinue or change the pill, for any reason, she must contact her doctor.*

## How is the pill taken?

It is very important that the pill be taken daily. Birth control pills come in monthly packs. The combination pill usually comes in 28-day packs. The first twenty-one pills are active pills that contain synthetic hormones to prevent pregnancy. The other seven pills, from the twenty-second to the twenty-eigth day are reminder pills and contain no hormones. The reminder pills should be taken, and after a woman completes the 28-day pack, she should start the new pack.

The combination pill is also available in 21-day packs. All the pills are active and are taken for twenty-one consecutive days. The woman waits seven days before she begins the next 21-day pack. Most doctors do not like the 21-day pack because women often forget to start the new pack after seven days, putting her at risk for pregnancy.

The Progestin pill comes in 28-day packages only. Each of the twenty-eight pills contain active hormones.

When taken correctly, the pill is extremely effective, with less than 2% chance of pregnancy.

## What time of day should the pill be taken?

The pill can be taken any time of the day, but should be taken *at the same time every day*. A woman should choose a time that is easy to remember and suits her lifestyle.

Many patients take the pill in the morning just after brushing their teeth.

## When should the pill be started?

The pill can be started on a Sunday or on the first day of menstruation. If a woman starts the pill on a Sunday and is a first-time user, she should use another form of birth control for the first seven days, such as a diaphragm, condom, spermicidal cream or jelly. Starting the next pack the day after the first 28-day pack is completed is necessary, regardless of whether or nor the menstrual period has taken place. If menstruation does not occur, however, the doctor should be notified.

If you choose to start the pill on the first day of your period it must be taken within twenty-four hours of the start of the period. If this is done, you will be protected against pregnancy immediately.

## Reordering the pill

Many women get nervous when they find that they have finished the pills, but cannot get a prescription immediately. To avoid this, the doctor should be informed about the refill at least one week prior to the date the pack will run out. If the next pack is not started on time, the patient may experience irregular bleeding and a higher risk of pregnancy.

# CHAPTER 10

## Intrauterine Devices

## Overview

### What is an intrauterine device (IUD)?

An IUD is a device that is inserted into the uterus to prevent pregnancy. It is the most commonly used form of reversible birth control in the world.

IUDs have received a lot of negative publicity over the years, as a result of a lawsuit against the makers of the Dalkon Shield, a specific type of IUD that was alleged to have caused a high number of pelvic infections. Consequently, many pharmaceutical companies stopped selling IUDs altogether, and many doctors stopped prescribing them.

Although most doctors believe strongly in the safety and effectiveness of the new and improved IUDs on the market, the stigma has persisted in the US. American women rarely seriously consider IUDs when evaluating birth control options. In fact, just 1% of women in the United States use an IUD compared to about one quarter of European women. However, American women rely heavily on methods of birth control that involve surgery or taking daily pills. According to the 1995 National Survey of Family Growth, 28% of women surveyed had undergone tubal sterilization, 27% used birth control pills, and 11% relied on their partners having had a vasectomy (male sterilization). This underutilization of the IUD prevents many women from experiencing the significant benefits that are specific to this method of birth control. Unlike tubal ligation, which is generally considered irreversible, the IUD (once removed) is unlikely to impede pregnancy. In addition, it does not require surgery and its long-term use can greatly reduce the cost of birth control.

## Types of IUDs

Three types of IUDs are currently marketed in the US:

- Paraguard T380A can be used for approximately eight to ten years and has a failure rate of less than 1%.

- Progestasert, which releases progesterone, has to be changed every year and also has a failure rate of less than 1%.

- The failure rate of Mirena is also less than 1%. All of these IUDs become effective immediately after they are inserted into the uterus.

## Cost of an IUD

- The cost of an IUD, which includes an examination and a follow-up visit, is about $600.

- If the long-acting IUD is kept in place for ten years, the yearly cost is only about $60. *(In comparison the average yearly cost of using birth control pills is more than $300.)*

## How do IUDs prevent pregnancy?

Doctors and scientists are still unsure exactly why and how IUDs work. Some theorize that it prevents the sperm from moving to the mouth of the womb and into the fallopian tubes. Others think that the IUD rushes the movement of the egg through the fallopian tubes.

We do know that the copper in the Paraguard changes the enzymes that are present in the lining of the womb. Progestasert, which contains progestin, is believed to thicken the cervical mucus and interfere with the movement of sperm. It also affects the lining of the uterus, which prevents implantation. Mirena releases small quantities of a hormone called Levonorgestrel,

## Intrauterine Device (IUD)

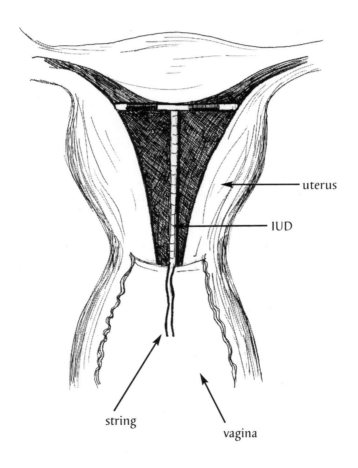

uterus

IUD

string

vagina

which stops the ovaries from releasing the egg, alters the lining in the womb and also thickens the cervical mucus to stop the sperm from moving forward.

## Who is a good candidate for the IUD?

The best candidate for the IUD is a woman who wants a long-term form of birth control, who already has children and is in a mutually monogamous relationship. She should have no history of pelvic infections. This method is suitable for women who do not want or are not yet ready for tubal ligation, but want a long-term contraceptive. More mature women, who are more likely to be in a stable relationship, usually prefer IUDs. It is extremely important that sexual partners be monogamous if the IUD is chosen as a contraceptive, because IUDs do not protect against sexually transmitted diseases (STDs).

## Women who should not use the IUD:

- women with confirmed or suspected pregnancies,

- women with a previous history of pelvic infections,

- women with conditions that increase their risk for infection (such as AIDS, diabetes, and IV drug users),

- women who are on prescribed steroids,

- women with cervical cancer,

- women who are allergic to copper,

- women who have Wilson's disease,

- women who have more than one sexual partner,

- women with undiagnosed vaginal bleeding,

- women who have an active infection of the uterus following childbirth or abortion,

- women with a "short uterus," and

- women with breast cancer.

## Before the IUD is inserted

Before an IUD is inserted, women should undergo a through medical examination, during which the doctor may check for vaginal infections or STDs. Doctors usually provide their patients with a consent form, explaining the side effects and the risks of the IUD. Before signing this form, a patient should have a thorough understanding of these factors. (This holds true for all other birth control methods as well, where it is equally important for women to read and understand the package insert prior to use.) Because IUDs do not protect against STDs, it is extremely important that both partners are confident about the exclusivity of their sexual relationship.

## Timing the insertion of the IUD

Most doctors insert the IUD during a woman's menstrual period to be sure that there is no risk of pregnancy. Also, the menstrual fluid acts as a lubricant, facilitating the insertion.

## Insertion of IUD

Initially, a speculum examination is done, and the mouth of the womb is held with a tenaculum to steady the womb, causing the woman to feel a slight pinch. The doctor then inserts a small instrument to measure the size of the womb. The IUD is inserted inside the uterus with a small plunger. Once inside the uterus, the arms of the T-shaped IUD opens up. The strings that come out beneath the T are trimmed to about 1-½ inches.

The doctor usually counsels women about the potential side effects of the IUD, such as continuous cramping for the first few days or weeks after insertion. Other side effects include increased menstrual pain and bouts of heavy bleeding. The doctor may prescribe medication to ease the symptoms or discomfort of such side effects. It is essential for women to be aware of exactly what kind of IUD they are using, so they know when it should be removed or replaced.

It is also vital that women check the string of the IUD regularly. When the IUD is inserted, the doctor will explain how to check the string. Women who are especially anxious about preventing pregnancy should check the string weekly. The string can be felt by inserting the index and middle finger into the vagina and finding the cervix, which feels something like the tip of the nose. Women should be able to feel the string in front of the cervix. It is important to feel the string in place to confirm that the IUD is positioned correctly. If no string is felt, the doctor should be notified immediately. It is possible for the IUD to be expelled from a woman's body without her being aware of it.

## Timing the removal of the IUD

The IUD can be removed anytime by a doctor, who holds the string with a special instrument and carefully pulls it out. Another IUD can be replaced at the same time the existing IUD is removed. In rare instances, if the doctor cannot find the string, a sonogram or an X-ray is done to search for the IUD. Sometimes the IUD is found inside the woman's womb. If this happens, the woman is given local anesthesia, the mouth of the womb is opened, and the IUD is removed. It rarely happens that the IUD will not come out when the string is pulled and the woman must be given general anesthesia to remove the IUD. It is also possible, but unlikely, for the IUD to perforate the uterus and go into the abdomen.

## Patient counseling and education

Women should contact their doctor, if there are any signs of infection or if the string is displaced. An IUD-related infection will cause such symptoms as fever, pain and foul-smelling discharge. Women should also inform their doctor if they experience unusual vaginal bleeding, a missed or late period, severe pain or cramps, lightheadedness or abnormal discharge.

## Potential side effects of IUDs

- **Change in menstrual periods:** The IUD can change the menstrual bleeding pattern. Women with heavy menstrual periods should tell their doctor, as this can be a factor in choosing an appropriate IUD.

- **Pain during menstruation:** Pain during menstruation can increase as a result of the IUD. The cramps are usually alleviated by over-the-counter medications.

- **Pelvic infection:** IUDs increase the incidence

of pelvic infections in women. However, research has shown that the probability of infection for the three IUDs mentioned in this chapter is less than for the IUDs used fifteen years ago.

- **Decreased chance of pregnancy after removal:** Because the IUD can decrease the chance of future pregnancy, it is usually not appropriate for women who do not have children. However, it should be remembered that many, many women have had successful pregnancies after having used an IUD.

## Chance of pregnancy with IUD

Although the risk of becoming pregnant is less than 1% with any form of IUD, the exact statistic varies, depending on the type of IUD. The pregnancy can occur inside or outside of the uterus. When it occurs outside, it is usually in the fallopian tubes, which is known as ectopic pregnancy. This is a life-threatening condition that often requires surgery. If the pregnancy is inside of the uterus, there is increased risk of miscarriage, stillbirth and other complications. It is, therefore, very important for a woman to contact her doctor immediately, if she misses her period.

# Mirena

## What is Mirena?

Mirena is a new form of IUD, which was released in the United States in 2000. It releases small quantities of levonorgestrel and can be kept inside the uterus for five years. This IUD was first marketed in Finland in 1990, and for the last ten years it has been used in Europe.

## Cost of Mirena

- The average cost for insertion of this IUD and follow up visit is about $600.
- If it is kept for five years, the monthly cost is about $10.

## How does Mirena prevent pregnancy?

It is believed that it stops the ovaries from releasing the eggs, and it thickens the mucus around the mouth of the womb. It also alters the lining of the womb to prevent implantation.

## Effectiveness

- The chance of pregnancy is less than 1%. If one hundred women use this method for five years, chances are that less than one of them will get pregnant.

## Women who can use Mirena

Mirena is only appropriate for women who are in a stable, mutually monogamous relationship and are not worried about sexually transmitted diseases. The women should have at least one child and no history of pelvic inflammatory disease, which is an infection of the reproductive organs. Nor should she have a history of ectopic pregnancies, which is pregnancy that occurs outside the uterus.

## Women who should not use Mirena

Please read the chapter on Intrauterine Devices, including the section on women who should not use the IUD. Women who are allergic to levonorgestrel, silicon, polyethylene, or unable to take hormones should not use Mirena.

# CHAPTER 11

## *Condoms*

## Male Condoms

### What is a condom?

A condom is a thin sheet of latex or rubber, which is used to cover the penis during intercourse.

### How do condoms work?

Condoms are a barrier method of birth control. The physical barrier of the condom prevents the sperm from entering the woman's body and meeting the egg. The condom is put on an erect penis, before the penis is inserted into the woman's vagina. The condom must be carefully removed after sex to prevent the sperm from spilling out. The chance of pregnancy is further diminished when the condom is used with a spermicide,

Male Condom

which is found in contraceptive gels, creams, foams and suppositories. Plus, spermicides increase the effectiveness of the condom against some sexually transmitted disease (STDs).

## Why condoms are so important?

There are an estimated 15 million cases of STDs diagnosed each year and nearly 1 million cumulative cases of HIV in the United States. Abstinence is the best defense against HIV, other STDs and pregnancy. After abstinence, a latex condom, if used consistently and correctly, is the best way to prevent STDs, including HIV, chlamydia, human papilloma virus, and trichomoniasis.

Although, women tend to prefer hormonal birth control methods to prevent pregnancy, they must remember that such methods do not protect them from STDs. Regardless of what other method is used for birth control, *condoms should be used additionally to prevent the spread of STDs.*

## How should condoms be used?

A condom should be put on while the penis is erect. The condom is put on the head of the penis and rolled back to the base. The tip of the condom should be held between the fingers while it is being rolled back to prevent the top part from filling with air, which can cause the condom to burst.

After ejaculation the man should remove the condom while holding its base tightly. It should not be removed near the vagina. A new condom should be used for each sexual act and every form of sexual contact, and it should be used for the entire duration of each sexual act.

## Lubrication of the condom

Some women complain of vaginal pain during intercourse, resulting from the condom. In such cases, the outside of the condom should be lubricated to reduce vaginal friction. Oil-based lubricants, such as petroleum jelly or vegetable oil, should not be used, because they can weaken the condom, causing it to rupture. Only contraceptive foam or water-based lubricants should be used with condoms.

## Side effects

- Condoms can cause allergic reaction in some people,

- can leak or burst due to improper use, and

- can cause infection.

## Effectiveness

The pregnancy rate for couples using condoms is 10% – 15% per year. Although, most people believe that these pregnancies are a result of condom leakage or breakage, studies have revealed that less than 2% of condoms break. More than 50% of couples do not use condoms for every act of intercourse, and many use them incorrectly.

- Condoms can break, of course, but this usually is a result of incorrect application. It is vital while putting on the condom, that the tip be held to eliminate any balloon effect at the top.

- The U.S. Food and Drug Administration regulates the quality of condoms. Under their strict quality control rules, if more than 2.5% of a batch is not made of pure latex or 0.4% leak, the whole batch must be rejected.

- The rate of effective use of condoms appears to increase in relation to one's age and marital status.

## Types of condoms

- **Latex condoms:** These condoms are made from a particular variety of rubber. Scientists have found them highly effective in preventing the spread of HIV and other viruses.

- **Synthetic condoms:** Very few people have a known allergy to latex, but for those who do, condoms made out of polyurethane—soft plastic—can be used. There are other types of synthetic latex condoms, which are also effective barriers against pregnancy and STDs.

- **Lambskin condoms:** These condoms are made from animal membranes, they are not known to protect against STDS, though scientists believe that they can help prevent pregnancy.

- **Novelty condoms:** They are not "real" condoms and should not be used for preventing pregnancy or STDs.

- **Female condoms:** These are made of polyurethane and cover the inside and outside of the vagina. They help prevent pregnancy and some STDs.

## Cost and availability

- The cost for a plain condom is usually less than 50 cents.

- They are widely available without a prescription at supermarkets, drug stores and vending machines.

# Female Condoms

## What is a female condom?

This barrier method of birth control is a sheet, which is made up of thin, soft plastic that it is inserted in the vagina before intercourse. It is transparent and has two flexible rings. The end with the smaller ring is inserted into the vagina. The larger rings stays outside of the vagina to help protect the external genital area.

## How does it work?

It is a physical barrier to prevent sperm from entering the uterus.

## Effectiveness

- It is generally believed that the failure rate is about 20%.

## Female Condom

outer ring

inner ring

## Advantages

- Studies have shown that it gives some degree of protection against sexually transmitted diseases.

## Disadvantages

- It must be removed before the user stands up.

- It is more expensive than the male condoms.

- It can slip into the vagina during intercourse. In some women, it causes vaginal irritation.

## Cost

- The female condom costs from $2 to $3.

## Insertion of Female Condom

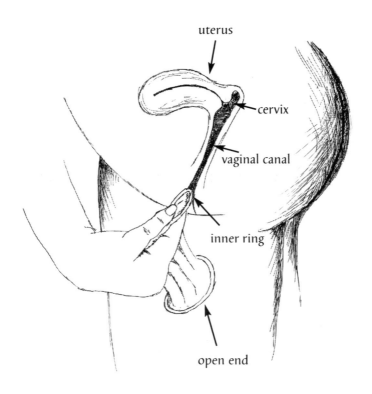

# Female Condom inside the Vagina

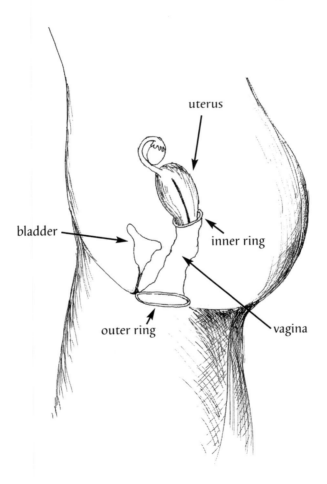

uterus

bladder

inner ring

outer ring

vagina

# CHAPTER 12

## *Spermicides*

### What are spermicides?

Spermicides are substances inserted into the vagina to prevent pregnancy. They come in different forms such as jelly, foam, cream, tablets and suppositories. Spermicides kill sperm on contact.

### How do they work?

The active ingredient present in the spermicide is nonoxynol-9, which damages the outer membrane of the sperm and incapacitates it, preventing pregnancy.

### How does one use a spermicide?

It is inserted prior to sexual intercourse. It is important that the spermicide is placed in front of the cervix, which feels like the tip of the nose. Women should read the patient labeling for correct use, as different products have different directions. Because spermicides come in different forms, women must follow the directions carefully for maximum effectiveness. Special directions includes waiting fifteen minutes for the spermicide to start working and inserting the spermicide with a vaginal applicator. The temperature of the body melts the spermicides, so most are only effective for one hour. For every act of intercourse, spermicide must be reapplied.

## Effectiveness

- For a typical patient, the failure rate is about 20%.

- If used correctly every time, the failure rate drops to about 6%.

- Using a male condom in conjunction with a spermicide is a good way to prevent not only pregnancy, but also many sexually transmitted diseases (STDs).

- It is crucial to reapply spermicide for every act of intercourse. In addition, women who use a diaphragm must also use a spermicide to lower the risk of pregnancy.

## Side Effects

- Side effects include itching, burning and irritation of the vaginal area and penis.

- Some researchers believe that it can cause vaginal infection.

## Pregnancy following use of spermicides

- Medical research has concluded that a baby conceived after a woman has used spermicides will not be affected.

## Advantages

- Spermicides are easily available without a prescription.

- Spermicides protect against some STDs.

- They increase vaginal lubrication, which helps some women.

## Disadvantages

- Spermicides can cause allergic reactions, vaginal infections or penile irritation.

## Costs

- Spermicides usually cost between $8 and $15.

# CHAPTER 13

## *Diaphragms*

### What is a diaphragm?

A diaphragm is a dome-shape soft rubber cup that covers the cervix, which is the mouth of the womb. It has a flexible ring, comes in various sizes, and is usually used with a spermicide.

### How does it work?

It acts as a physical barrier, preventing sperm form entering the uterus. Also, the spermicide used with it prevents the sperm from moving.

### How effective is it in preventing pregnancy?

If used properly, six couples in one hundred will become pregnant. However, usual rate of failure is 20%, which

### Diaphragm

### Diaphragm inside the vagina

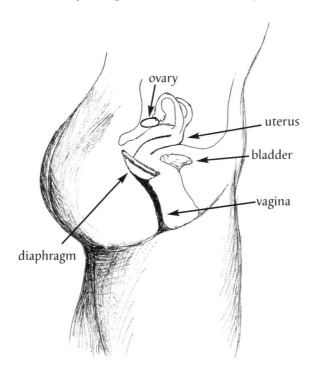

ovary

uterus

bladder

vagina

diaphragm

means that twenty females out of one hundred will get pregnant in one year.

The chances of pregnancy are decreased if the following things are done:

- The partner uses a condom.
- Contraceptive jelly is reapplied before intercourse is repeated.
- The diaphragm is properly fitted.
- The diaphragm is held up to the light to check for holes prior to each use.

## How does one get the diaphragm?

You must make an appointment with a doctor to request a diaphragm. The doctor will do an internal examination and assess what size diaphragm is needed. After determining the size, the doctor gives you a prescription. You then go to the pharmacy to get the diaphragm. Be sure to get a contraceptive foam or jelly with the diaphragm.

The sizes change after:

- pregnancy, or
- weight gain of more than ten pounds.

*Doctors teach patients how to correctly insert, remove, and take care of the diaphragm.*

## Insertion of the diaphragm

Hands must be washed first. The diaphragm should be held like a cup. Spermicides should be put in the center and around the rim of the diaphragm, and this is the side that should face the cervix when the diaphragm is in place. Position yourself comfortably, and fold the diaphragm in half and push it all the way into the vagina. It is very important that the diaphragm covers the cervix completely. You should put your finger inside the vagina and feel the rubber of the diaphragm covering the cervix. The cervix feels like the tip of the nose.

## Removal of the diaphragm

Hands must be washed first, and the patient can use any position that is comfortable for her. The finger should be hooked behind the rim of the diaphragm to gently pull out the diaphragm.

## Taking care of the diaphragm

Before each use, the diaphragm should be held up to the light to check for any holes. The diaphragm should be washed and dried after each use, and stored in a cool, dry place.

## Side effects

- The most common side effect is recurrent bladder infection.

- Vaginal itching, discharge or bleeding are also possible and should be reported to the doctor.

## Conditions when the doctor might not use the diaphragm

- The diaphragm cannot be inserted properly in patients who have very tight muscles.

- Also, if the vaginal muscles are very weak or there are cysts or obstruction of the vagina, the diaphragm cannot be used.

## Benefits of using the diaphragm

- The diaphragm, when used with spermicide, may offer protection against some sexually transmitted diseases.

- Women have control of its use, and if they use it correctly every time, the chance of pregnancy is six out of one hundred. The usual chance of pregnancy is twenty out of one hundred.

- It can be used with spermicide while breast-feeding.

## Disadvantages of the diaphragm

- You can get the diaphragm only by prescription.

- Some women have increased incidents of bladder infection after using the diaphragm.

- The diaphragm can slip out of position during sex.

- Some women have difficulty inserting the diaphragm.

- Some women have difficulty removing the diaphragm.

- Women need to be refitted for the diaphragm after pregnancy or after gaining more than ten pounds.

- The diaphragm cannot be removed immediately after intercourse. It must be kept for six hours afterward.

## Costs

- The office visit to the doctor costs around $60 to $125.

- The cost of the diaphragm is around $20.

- The approximate cost of contraceptive jelly or cream is $8 to $15.

# CHAPTER 14

## *NuvaRing*

### What is NuvaRing?

It is a flexible intravaginal ring, two inches in diameter and 1/8 of an inch thick, that releases 15 mcg of ethinyl estradiol and 120 mcg etonogestrel daily. (This new vaginal ring, approved by the Food and Drug Administration in 2001, will be available to the general market in 2002.)

### How does it work?

It works the same way as most birth control pills, preventing the release of the egg and thickening the cervical mucus to prevent sperm from going forward. The amount of hormones in the vaginal ring is lower than the amount present in the lowest-dose combination pill. The hormones are absorbed through the vagina into the body.

## How is it inserted?

It is inserted into the vagina on or before day five of the menstrual cycle and kept inside there for three weeks, at which point it is removed, to allow for menstruation. One week after removal, a new ring is inserted. Research has indicated that it prevents pregnancy for an entire month, including the week the ring is not in. It is made in only one size that fits all women and can be easily inserted and removed by the woman at home.

## Advantages

- The woman does not have to follow the daily routine of taking pills.

- It does not interfere with sex.

- The device is completely under the woman's control.

- There is no discomfort to the male partner.

- It is less bulky than the diaphragm and, because it is a one-size-fits-all product, it does not have to be fitted by a doctor.

- It causes less nausea and vomiting than birth control pills, because it is not taken orally, so the hormone bypasses the gastrointestinal system.

- It usually does not cause vaginal irritation.

## Disadvantages

- It has the same disadvantages as birth control pills, but the level of hormones released by the rings is the lowest of any combination birth control pills.

- It does not protect against sexually transmitted diseases.

## Effectiveness

- The failure rate is 1-2% per year.

## Costs

- Experts estimate that the cost for NuvaRing will be the same as a packet of birth control pills.

# CHAPTER 15

## Transdermal Contraception

### What is the patch?

Ortho-Evra is a transdermal patch, which is one of the newest birth control methods. It was approved by the Food and Drug Administration in 2001. It is manufactured by Ortho-McNeil Pharmaceutical Inc. and should be available in the second half of 2002. The patch offers women another birth control choice. It is very convenient to use. Many women find this birth control method suitable for their lifestyle. It is a reliable, effective and reversible form of birth control.

### How does it work?

The hormone patch releases a continuous flow of low amounts of estrogen and progestin. These hormones prevent ovulation.

## Who can use the patch?

Most women who can use the birth control pill can use the patch. It has been found that women weighing more than 198 pounds are not good candidates for the patch.

The contraceptive patch does not protect against HIV or other sexually transmitted diseases.

## When do you apply the patch?

The first patch should be applied on the first day of menstruation. This becomes the day of the week when the patch is changed. Women should apply a new patch weekly for three weeks followed by a break of one week.

Some women can apply the patch on the Sunday after the period has begun. It might be easier to remember Sunday. These women need back-up protection for 7 days when they use the patch for the first time.

## Where can you wear the patch?

The patch can be worn on the buttocks, abdomen, torso (excluding the breast), or the upper outer arm. Most women prefer to apply them on the abdomen or buttocks. Most patches adhere to the skin very well, even while swimming or doing exercise.

## Advantages

- Improved compliance

- The patch users were less likely to miss using the patch when compared with women who used birth control pills. The reason may be that the weekly schedule was easier to follow than the daily routine of taking birth control pills.

- One study showed that 90% of women used the patch properly compared to 80% of women who took the pills.

## Disadvantages

- A greater rate of pregnancy was noticed in women weighing over 198 pounds. (The patch might not provide adequate amounts of hormones to these women to prevent pregnancy.)

- Skin irritation.

- Incidents of bleeding increased during the first two menstrual cycles when compared to pill users.

- More breast discomfort during the first two cycles when compared to pill users.

## Failure rate

- The failure rate is less than 1%.

## Costs

- The cost has not been determined. It should be about the same price as a packet of birth control pills.

# CHAPTER 16

## Contraceptive Implants

### What is Norplant?

A Norplant implant consists of six plastic capsules (each the size of a match stick), filled with levonorgestrel. This is a long-acting contraceptive, which has to be inserted by a doctor and is usually placed under the skin of the upper arm.

### How long are they kept inside the body?

They are usually kept in for five years, but can be removed earlier. The reason that they are kept in for only five years is that the chance of pregnancy increases slightly in the sixth year.

## Norplant Capsules Inserted

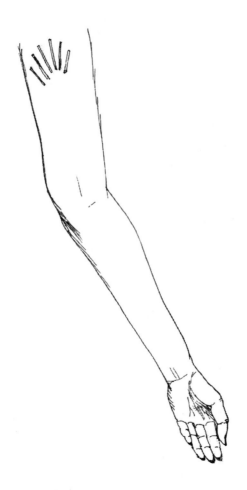

## Effectiveness

- This form of contraceptive is very effective, and the chance of pregnancy is less than 1%. If 1000 women use this form of birth control for one year, only eight will get pregnant.

- If a woman is overweight the chance of pregnancy is slightly higher. However, doctors still prescribe it for overweight women, because their chance of pregnancy using this method is still much lower than with other birth control methods.

## How does Norplant work?

Norplant works by preventing the ovary from releasing the egg. The cervical mucus, which is present at the entrance of the womb, thickens, thereby preventing the sperm from entering the womb.

## How do you get Norplant implants?

The first step is discussing it with your doctor. Norplant is inserted through a small incision, which is usually done in the doctor's office. First, the area where the Norplant will be inserted is cleaned with an antiseptic solution. Then, a local anesthetic is administered, and the implants are inserted through a small incision. There is slight discomfort after insertion, which usually goes away with ordinary pain medication. Women can resume work immediately after the insertion. Some patients have pain and swelling for a few days.

## Timing of the insertion

Doctors like to do the insertion within the first seven days from the start of the period. The reason for this is to ensure that the woman is not pregnant. However, it can be inserted at any time, as long as the woman is not pregnant.

For breastfeeding mothers, Norplant can be inserted six weeks after delivery. If the mother is not breastfeeding, it can be done immediately after delivery.

## Time required for Norplant to become effective

It is believed that it becomes effective after eight hours.

## Removal of the implants

The implant is usually removed after five years, but it can be removed anytime the woman wants. The discomfort during removal is slightly more than with insertion, because implants sometimes get lodged in the tissue. Fertility returns within one week after removal.

## Side effects

- The most important side effect is the changes in the menstrual period. Most women experience irregular bleeding during the first year. If a woman cannot cope with irregular bleeding, she is not a candidate for this implant. However, when patients are counseled well about this side effect, they are better able to cope with the bleeding.

- Some women complain about the absence of their period. Studies have shown that 10% of women using Norplant will have absent periods, within the five-year period. In addition, headaches are sometimes a problem for women.

## Benefits

- This is a good long-term contraceptive.
- It does not interfere with having sex,
- it does not have to be taken daily and
- breastfeeding mothers can use it six weeks after delivery.

## Disadvantages

- It does not prevent HIV or any other sexually transmitted diseases.
- Bleeding is a problem during the first year.
- Insertion and removal are small operations that cause some discomfort.

## Cost

- Office visit with insertion of the Norplant is around $400 to $500.
- Removal cost is about $250.

# CHAPTER 17

## Injectable Contraceptives

### What are injectable contraceptives?

These are contraceptives that are given by injection either in the arms or buttocks. They are called Depoprovera and Lunelle.

## Depoprovera

### What is Depoprovera?

This is the only contraceptive injection available at the present time, besides Lunelle. It is a reversible form of birth control that acts like progesterone in the human body. It is only available by prescription. It is commonly known as "the shot."

## How does Depoprovera prevent pregnancy?

It prevents pregnancy by preventing the ovaries from releasing eggs. Depoprovera also thickens the mucus near the mouth of the womb, which prevents the sperm from moving inside.

## What are the benefits?

- It is a very effective form of birth control that has to be taken only once every three months, making it less of a "hassle" to women.
- Also, it does not have to be taken daily and does not interfere while having sex.
- In some patients, Depoprovera reduces vaginal bleeding and cramps.
- A distinct advantage is that it can be used while breastfeeding.
- Patients who cannot take estrogen can take Depoprovera.

## Side effects

- In many women, Depoprovera causes changes in the menstrual cycle. A small percentage of women experience bleeding, and some patients spot continuously. It may take six months to one year for menstrual periods to resume after the last injection.

- Some women experience increased appetite and weight gain. Others complain of painful breast, and a small percentage of women experience depression.

## What you should discuss with your doctor before you take Depoprovera?

You should tell the doctor if you are pregnant or want to become pregnant in the next twelve to eighteen months. In women who want to be on depoprovera most doctors tell them that after the injections are stopped, it usually takes twelve to eighteen months to get pregnant. Your doctor should know if the possibility of irregular vaginal bleeding bothers you a lot. You should not take this if you have serious liver disease, breast cancer or are allergic to the medication. The doctor should be informed if you have any history of diabetes, depression or blood clots. If, after you have taken the shot, you experience continuous vaginal bleeding, depression, pain in the abdomen or any other abnormal symptoms, you should notify your doctor.

## When to take the shot?

Usually, the injection is given in the first week after your period starts. If you are not breastfeeding, it can be given soon after birth. For breastfeeding mothers, it is advisable to wait for six weeks after birth.

The injection must be repeated after twelve weeks. If you are more than two weeks late for the shot, you should do a pregnancy test.

## Costs

- The cost of the medication is between $40 to $75. The doctor visit is about $60 to $125.

# Lunelle

## What is Lunelle?

It is a birth control medication containing estrogen and progesterone, which is given as a shot.

## How does it work?

It changes the lining of the womb, thus preventing the fertilized egg from implanting. It also prevents the ovary from releasing the egg. Many researchers think that it also thickens the mucus around the mouth of the womb to prevent sperm from reaching the egg.

## Failure rate of Lunelle

- Less than one out of one hundred women using this contraceptive for one year will get pregnant.

## Best candidates for Lunelle

This birth control method is suitable for women who do not want the inconvenience of taking pills daily, prefer regular periods and want a method that is easily reversible. The Depoprovera injection, which is given every three months, is not quickly reversible, which gives Lunelle a distinct advantage.

## Benefits of Lunelle

- It is believed that the injection has the same benefits as birth control pills. However, because this method has not been on the market for very long, this belief has not been proven over time.

- It has the advantage of decreased menstrual bleeding and cramping during periods, and studies show that it can help regulate womens' periods.

## Contra-indications

The contra-indications are the same as birth control pills. *(Please read the chapter on birth control pills.)*

## Disadvantages of Lunelle

- It has the same side effects as birth control pills.
- *(Please read the section on side effects in the chapter on birth control pills.)*
- Review the package insert and patient labeling carefully before using this medication.

## Cost of Lunelle

- The cost of Lunelle is around $35 per month.

# CHAPTER 18

## *Withdrawal*

### What is withdrawal?

It is a method by which a man withdraws his penis from the woman's vagina just before reaching climax and ejaculates away from her vagina. It is also known as coitus interruptus.

### How does it work?

It prevents the sperm from entering the vagina, thus preventing pregnancy.

### Effectiveness

- The failure rate is about 25%.

## Advantages

- It does not require any medication or devices.
- It is permitted by some religions that forbid other methods.
- It has no medical side effects.

## Disadvantages

- The chance of pregnancy is very high and it requires self control by the man.
- It does not protect against HIV or any other sexually transmitted disease and
- reduces sexual satisfaction.

## People who are advised not to use the method

- Men who lack the self control to pull out the penis in time
- Teenagers
- Men who cannot determine when they will ejaculate

# Part Three

*Irreversible Methods*

# CHAPTER 19

## *Sterilization*

## Tubal Sterilization

### What is tubal sterilization?

Tubal sterilization is often referred to as "tying the tubes" or "tubal ligation." In this birth control method, the fallopian tubes can be clamped, cut, tied or cauterized.

### How does it work?

This procedure blocks the passage of the fallopian tubes, which stops the sperm from reaching the egg, thereby preventing pregnancy.

### Effectiveness

The chance of pregnancy after tubal ligation is less than

one in one hundred. One out of three pregnancies that do occur after tubal ligation is in the fallopian tubes (ectopic pregnancy).

## When should you consider sterilization?

When you and your partner have decided that your family is complete, and you do not want any more children. This is a very important decision and should be considered irreversible. If there is even the slightest possibility that you will want to get pregnant later, you should not choose tubal sterilization. Rather, you should talk to your doctor to choose another method of birth control after assessing their effectiveness, safety and reversibility.

You might have heard about surgery for reversing sterilization. This operation is complicated, expensive and not always successful. Currently, most tubal ligation is done through a laparoscope, and the tubes are burned, reducing the chance of successful reversal.

You need to be completely sure about how you feel before making this decision. Serious consideration must be given to your future reproductive life to ensure that you do not regret your decision later in life, regardless of the future status of your current family.

Many women are choosing tubal sterilization, because the cost of birth control is high and not always covered by medical insurance. Tubal ligation, on the other hand, is covered by medical insurance. While tubal ligation does enable women to avoid the recurring expenses of most birth control methods, the decision to opt for a procedure with such extreme—and likely permanent—consequences should not be based solely on the financial considerations. If money is a major factor affecting your birth control decision, and you are not comfortable with the idea of sterilization, please read the chapter on "Reducing the Cost of Birth Control," and talk to your physician to find a birth control method that suits you and your budget.

## Alternative birth control methods

If you want a choice of birth control that is as effective as tubal ligation but reversible, you can choose from birth control pills, Depoprovera, Norplant and intrauterine devices. All of these have very few serious side effects. Another option is using a diaphragm and condom together. Unlike tubal ligation and vasectomy, these methods are reversible, and when used appropriately, carry a very low risk of serious complications.

Vasectomy is another option that you can discuss with your partner. Vasectomy, or male sterilization, is much simpler and cheaper than tubal ligation.

## Misconceptions about sterilization

Sterilization does not affect femininity or decrease sexual desire. Many patients ask: "What will happen to the egg?" It is simply absorbed in the body, and there is little change in the menstrual period.

Although you do not need your partner's consent for sterilization, you will always be advised to discuss it with your partner. Sterilization cannot be forced by anybody.

Single women without children can be sterilized at their own request, if they know that they never want children.

## Chances of pregnancy after tubal ligation

Women should be aware that there is a chance of pregnancy and ectopic pregnancy (pregnancy in the fallopian tubes) after tubal ligation. The chance of pregnancy after tubal ligation is less than one in one hundred. The symptoms of ectopic pregnancy are absence of the period, spotting and abdominal pain, possibly in conjunction with fainting spells. If you have any suspicion that you might have an ectopic pregnancy go to the emergency room immediately.

# Types of sterilization

## Laparoscopy

This procedure is usually done under general anesthesia in a hospital or surgery center. An incision about 1 cm long is made in the belly button, a needle is inserted into the abdomen and a small amount of gas is infused to distend the abdomen. Then, a telescope-like instrument, called a laparoscope, is inserted into the abdomen. The laparoscope is illuminated and connected to a video camera, so the pelvic organs can be viewed on a video screen. Other instruments are introduced through small incisions and the tube is cauterized, ligated, or cinched with a ring or a band to block the passageway. After the surgery, the gas is expelled, and the incision is closed with stitches.

## Mini Laparotomy

This operation is usually done under general anesthesia. It may be done in the hospital, after the birth of a baby, by making an incision under the belly button, and cutting, tying and removing segments of the tubes.

Occasionally, if the patient does not want a laparoscopy, a small incision is made on the lower abdomen, through which the tubes are tied and cut. This is only done if the patient is not pregnant.

# Laparoscopic Tubal Ligation

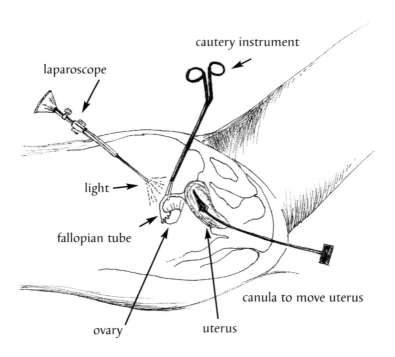

# Tubal Ligation

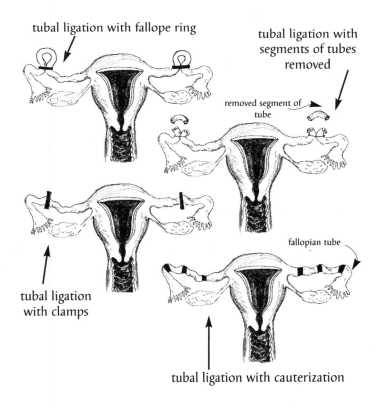

tubal ligation with fallope ring

tubal ligation with segments of tubes removed

removed segment of tube

tubal ligation with clamps

fallopian tube

tubal ligation with cauterization

## Complications of surgery

Complications are infection, bleeding, injury to bowel, bladder or other abdominal structures. They can also include side effects from the anesthesia and injury to blood vessels and nerves. The procedure has a failure rate of less than 1%.

## Vaginal procedures

Some doctors do tubal sterilization through an incision made in the vagina. This procedure, known as colpotomy, also requires cutting, tying and removing a segment of the tubes.

## Discomfort after operation

- Usually, there is moderate soreness after the operation.

- Women sometimes feel weak and have slight abdominal pain.

- If a fever, severe abdominal pain, nausea, vomiting or any other unexpected symptoms develop, the patient should contact her doctor.

## Cost of tubal ligation

- The approximate cost of tubal sterilization is $2,000 to $3,000.

# Vasectomy

## What is vasectomy?

Vasectomy is the sterilization of a man. It is the male equivalent of tubal ligation. However, because the vas deferens is just below the skin of the scrotum, as opposed to the fallopian tubes, which are inside of a woman's abdomen, sterilization is much more complicated for women than for men. In addition, vasectomy is less expensive, less painful, and carries less risk than tubal ligation. Many men agree to the procedure, once these points are properly explained to them, and any misconceptions they have regarding the after-effects of the procedure are dispelled. Each year, about 500,000 men undergo vasectomy, the most effective form of birth control for men.

## How does it work?

During vasectomy, the vas deferens—the passageway for the sperm to pass from the testes to the penis—is cut, clamped, or sealed.

The operation does not interfere with sexual pleasure or erection, and the amount of ejaculate remains the same. The difference is that there is not any sperm in the ejaculate. Vasectomy does not make a man impotent or decrease his masculinity.

## Appropriate candidates for vasectomy

Men who want to undergo vasectomy should agree with the following statements:

- You and your partner feel that your family is complete.

- You do not want more children.

- You want to spare your partner the pain and suffering of tubal ligation.

- All other options of birth control have been discussed with you and your partner.

Couples need to understand that this is a *permanent and irreversible* procedure. If there is any chance that a man might want to father a baby in the future, he should not undergo vasectomy. He should be sure that he would not regret this decision to choose vasectomy, even if his family situation changes.

## Vasectomy

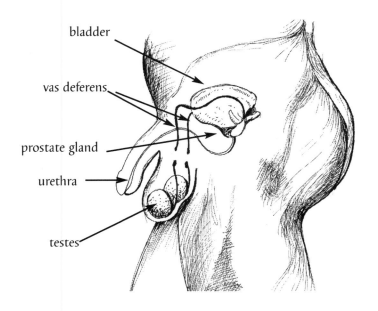

bladder

vas deferens

prostate gland

urethra

testes

Often men choose vasectomy, because the procedure is covered by a medical insurance policy that won't cover the cost of birth control pills and other contraceptive methods. High out-of-pocket expenses for birth control and fear of unintended pregnancy can greatly influence a couple's decision to opt for sterilization. Accordingly, it is not surprising that sterilization is among the most common methods of birth control in the United States.

## Procedure

Vasectomy is usually performed in a doctor's office by a urologist or family practitioner.

Using the fingers, the skin under the scrotum is lifted, and a local anesthetic is injected. A small nick is made on the skin, the vas deferens is held, tied and cut, or cauterized, and sometimes blocked with a clip. Using the "No Scalpel Method," the same procedure is performed through a puncture rather than a cut, which results in much less pain and fewer complications.

Vasectomy usually causes slight to moderate pain and swelling, which is easily treated with over-the-counter pain medication and ice bags.

## Reversal of vasectomy

This operation is quite complicated, with limited success. So, the decision of vasectomy should not be taken lightly.

## Risk of pregnancy immediately after vasectomy

Men do not become sterile immediately after vasectomy. Sperm may be collected in the part of the vas deferens that is distal to the block or cut. It takes about five to twenty ejaculations for this sperm to clear out completely. The doctor will repeat a sperm test until there is no evidence of sperm, at which point the couple can stop using other birth control methods.

## Failure rate

- The failure rate for vasectomy is about .2%.

## What happens to the sperm?

The body absorbs the sperm.

## Vasectomy and other health problems

- Studies have shown that there are no increased health risks for men, following vasectomy.

## Cost

- The cost is usually about $500 to $1000, including follow-up visits.

# Part Four

## *Fertility Awareness Methods*

# CHAPTER 20

## Rhythm Method

### What is the rhythm method?

This method uses the menstrual cycle to calculate a safe period when having intercourse will not result in pregnancy. A woman keeps a record of her menstrual cycle, and she and her partner agree not to have sex during the fertile period.

It is believed that sperm live for two to three days, and eggs live for three to four days. For a woman with a 28-day cycle, the day that bleeding starts is considered the first day of her cycle. Women normally ovulate in the middle of the cycle, which is the fourteenth day. So, the first ten days after the start of the period and the last ten days before the start of the next period are deemed "safe." However, there are variations, and many doctors believe that to be truly safe, couples should not have unprotected sex between day seven to day twenty-one of the cycle. *(Before you try this method, please discuss it with your doctor.)*

While the rhythm method works for some couples, it fails for many others. In order to be sure, a conventional contraceptive must be used.

## Advantages

- It does not require medication or devices, and
- it is permitted by some religions that forbid other types of birth control.
- It does not have side effects or interfere with lovemaking.
- It also does not cost anything.

## Disadvantages

- The couple needs to practice self-control and keep careful records.
- It does not protect from HIV and other sexually transmitted diseases.
- This method cannot be used by women with irregular periods.

## Failure rates

- The failure rate is approximately 20%.
  Therefore most doctors advise to combine the
  rhythm method, the cervical mucus method
  and the basal body temperature method.

## Cost

- $-0-

# CHAPTER 21

## Basal Body
## Temperature Method

### What is the basal body temperature method?

Like the rhythm method, this is a method involving fertility awareness. Pregnancy is prevented by using a woman's body temperature to determine her fertile period. It is based on the principal that just prior to ovulation (releasing the egg), body temperature drops a few tenths of a degree. After ovulation the temperature rises by 0.4 to 1.0 degrees Fahrenheit or 0.2 to 0.5 degrees Centigrade and does not go back to the pre-ovulatory temperature until the next period starts. *(Please consult with your doctor before trying this method.)*

Body temperature is lowest upon awakening, before any movement, so patients are advised to take their oral temperature before getting out of bed. A basal body temperature thermometer should be used, because it has an expanded scale that is easier to read.

The temperature should be taken with the mouth closed and should be recorded on a chart.

## How do you know the fertile period?

Women must record their daily body temperatures for several months to determine the exact time of ovulation during their cycle. They should avoid intercourse or use a back-up method during the first half of the cycle and for at least three days after the temperature has risen. The temperature usually rises by 0.4-1.0 degrees Fahrenheit or .2-.5 degrees Centigrade. After ovulation, body temperature should be higher than it is for the first half of the cycle.

## Advantages

- It does not require any medication or devices and
- it is permitted by some religions that forbid other types of birth control.
- It has no side effects and
- does not interfere with lovemaking.

## Disadvantages

- The risk of pregnancy is high, and

- it takes time to learn the method.

- It requires careful record keeping and self-control to abstain from sex during the fertile period.

- It does not prevent HIV and other sexually transmitted diseases.

## Failure rate

- The failure rate using this method alone is about 20%, so many doctors advise combining the basal body temperature method, the cervical mucus method and the rhythm method.

- Illness and staying up all night can both interfere with the temperature method.

## Costs

- The cost of the temperature kit is usually less than $8.

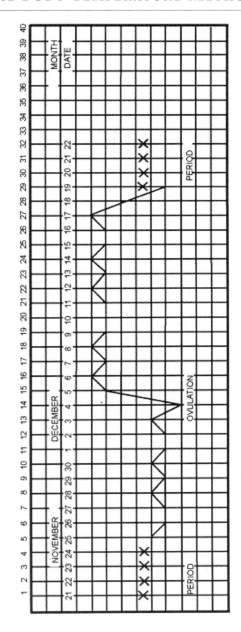

Basal Body Temperature Chart

# CHAPTER 22

## Cervical Mucus Method

### What is the cervical mucus method?

This fertility awareness method relies on monitoring changes in the amount and thickness of vaginal mucus to determine ovulation. When a finger is inserted into and then removed from the vagina after menstruation, there will be some evidence of mucus. Holding the mucus between the index finger and the thumb, the mucus should be stretched out in a strand. During ovulation, this strand can be stretched to about six inches before breaking. Women must chart and record their daily observations. *(Before you try this method, please discuss it with your doctor.)*

### When is a woman fertile?

A woman is fertile in the days surrounding ovulation. Prior to ovulation, the vagina is wet and there is evidence of mucus. Slowly, the mucus increases becoming most abundant during ovulation. After ovulation, the mucus decreases or goes away altogether. If a woman monitors her mucus for several months, she will be able to gauge when she is ovulating.

## Effectiveness

- Although for some women this method is effective, for many it is not.
- It is sometimes difficult to gauge the amount of mucus.
- The presence of spermicide and douching will change the mucus.
- Vaginal infections interfere with this method.

## Characteristics of mucus

- During ovulation, the mucus is clear and thin and can be stretched six to eight inches before breaking.
- Prior to ovulation, the mucus is a mixture of clear and cloudy and can be stretched only slightly.
- A few days after ovulation, the mucus again becomes slightly thicker, but stretches only four to five inches.

# Cervical Mucus Method

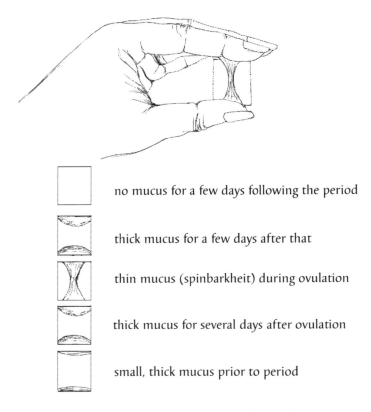

no mucus for a few days following the period

thick mucus for a few days after that

thin mucus (spinbarkheit) during ovulation

thick mucus for several days after ovulation

small, thick mucus prior to period

- Before the period, the mucus is thick but scanty.

- After the period, the mucus is scanty to nonexistent. The amount of mucus slowly increases as a woman gets further into her cycle, but it cannot be stretched until just prior to ovulation.

## Disadvantages

- The risk of pregnancy is high, if the method is not properly practiced.
- It might be difficult to determine the safe period.
- The couple must exercise self-control.
- It does not prevent HIV or other sexually transmitted diseases.

## Advantages

- It does not require any medication or device.
- It has no side effects, and it is permitted by some religions that forbid other forms of birth control.
- It does not interfere with lovemaking.
- It does not cost anything.

## Failure rate

Approximately 20% using this method alone. Therefore, many doctors advise combining the basal body temperature method, the cervical mucus method and the rhythm method.

## Cost

- $-0-

# CHAPTER 23

## Sexually Transmitted Diseases: An Overview

Sexually transmitted diseases (STDs) are infections, which are transmitted from one person to another through sexual contact. STDs are also known as sexually transmitted infections, reproductive tract infections or venereal diseases. One out of every four people has an STD and there are more than twenty known STDs that can be spread through vaginal, oral, or anal sex. Each year more than 15 million Americans are infected with an STD. The annual cost for treating STDs in the U.S. is 10 to 15 billion dollars. The Center for Disease Control and Prevention states that the problem of STDs has reached epidemic proportions now.

## The most common questions asked about STDs include:

- What are the types of STDs?

- How long does it take from the time of the initial exposure to develop an STD?

- What are the symptoms?

- How do people contract an STD?

- How can people protect themselves?

- How are STDs diagnosed?

- Can an STD prevent a woman from getting pregnant?

- What is the medical treatment?

- What happens if an STD is left untreated?

The commonly known STDs are: chlamydia, HIV, gonorrhea, herpes, human papilloma virus, genital warts, syphilis, trichomoniasis, and hepatitis B, but there are other, lesser known STDs as well.

## Why STDs are so common

The number of STD cases has been rising rapidly each year. The following are some of the reasons behind this epidemic:

- Most people do not understand how prevalent STDs are and don't know how to protect themselves.

- Teenagers are becoming sexually active at an earlier age, and people are getting married at a later age. Nearly 60% of STDs occur in people younger than 25 years old.

- More than 50% of marriages end in divorce.

- Many people have multiple sex partners.

- There is also very little serious discussion about the problem in the media.

- Many people believe that it is only a problem among prostitutes and their clientele.

- Many people believe, mistakenly, that it is only a problem among the people of the lower socioeconomic classes. Not true. This is a problem throughout the country, in every type of neighborhood and every socioeconomic class.

- Many people ignore the subject out of a sense of shame or embarrassment. Teenagers are especially uncomfortable talking to their doctor or family about STDs.

- Since most STDs cause no immediate symptoms, one person can infect the other through sexual contact without even realizing it. In women, the symptoms can be confusing, so they are often ignored or diagnosed after there is already permanent damage. Regular medical check-ups and testing to diagnose these diseases early helps prevent such damage and hinder the spread of STDs.

• Young teenage girls are especially susceptible to contracting STDs, because their vaginal tissue is weaker and more vulnerable to infection.

## The Effects of STDs

STDs can have grave health consequences. The effects of STDs range from the simple annoyance of vaginal discharge to death from HIV.

STDs can also result in infertility. Infections like gonorrhea or chlamydia can spread through the uterus to the fallopian tubes and leave the tubes blocked by scar tissue. Scar tissue can prevent sperm or an egg from moving through the tubes, thereby preventing conception. Scarring may also block an embryo from entering the uterus, causing a pregnancy in the fallopian tube, known as an ectopic pregnancy. This is a life-threatening condition, which can rupture the fallopian tube and cause severe bleeding. Ectopic pregnancies require immediate surgery.

STDs can affect people in a number of other ways as well. The Herpes virus can cause frequent recurring sores and ulcers; Human Papilloma virus can cause cancer of the cervix; and HIV can ultimately cause death. In addition, some STDs can be transferred from a pregnant mother to her unborn child inside the womb, resulting in congenital birth defects or even the death of the baby.

## Symptoms of STDs

Most people with STDs do not show any symptoms ,initially. STDs usually start in the genital area. For women, the infection often starts inside the vagina or on the vulva. For men, it usually starts in the penis, causing an abnormal discharge or blisters. Women may experience such symptoms as foul-smelling vaginal discharge, pain in the abdomen, and irregular bleeding. Both men and women may experience painful urination.

## What to do if you think you have an STD

Get help from your doctor or healthcare provider as soon as possible. Many clinics offer free testing for STDs. Testing is essential to determine the presence of an STD. Early diagnosis and treatment is extremely important for both partners. It can prevent permanent physical damage and can even save a life.

# CHAPTER 24

## Prevention of Sexually Transmitted Diseases

Preventing sexually transmitted diseases (STDs) is crucial to good health. Many infections do not produce symptoms in the early stages, making them difficult to detect. In these cases, by the time the infection is diagnosed, there may be permanent damage. One in four people has an STD.

It is much easier to prevent STDs than to cure them, and the best way to prevent them is ABSTINENCE. Even using a latex condom does not guarantee complete protection from STDs.

To reduce the risk of contacting STDs, all types of high risk sexual behavior should be eliminated. This includes having multiple sexual partners or having unprotected sex with someone who does. Having sex with an IV drug user or sharing needles also increases the risk of getting HIV and other STDs.

## How to Protect Yourself From STDs:

- **Have a monogamous relationship.** If you and your partner both have a monogamous relationship, it is unlikely that either of you will contract an STD. Do not be afraid to talk openly with your partner about this. The more partners you have or your partner has, the greater your risk for contracting an STD.

- **Know you partner well.** Be sure that your partner does not have an STD. If there are any sores, rashes or discharge, discuss this with your partner and advise the person to get medical attention. However, be aware that your partner could have an STD, but not know it or display any symptoms. If your partner has a contagious disease, you can contract it by having unprotected sex with the person even one time. Don't be shy about asking your partner about previous illnesses or checking your partner for signs of disease. Remember that your health depends on it.

- **Use latex condoms.** Use of latex condoms is very important in protecting you and your partner from STDs. When used correctly every time, condoms are one of the most effective barriers to STDs.

- **Healthcare providers usually recommend using a condom to prevent STDs** and another more reliable method to prevent pregnancy. Women should carry condoms with them, if they think that they might face an unpredictable situation.

- **Get regular check-ups.** Regular check-ups are very important for the early diagnosis of STDs. If you think that there is even a remote chance that you might have an STD, talk to your healthcare provider and request an STD test. Don't be embarrassed about confiding in your doctor about your suspicions or concerns. Your doctor is there to help you and will be happy that you are taking an active role in caring for your health.

- **Be honest with your partner.** If you are infected with an STD, you should inform your partner or partners and urge them to get tested and treated. Early treatment will help protect the health of your partner.

- **Use spermicides.** Spermicides containing Nonoxynol 9 help prevent the spread of some STDs. When used in conjunction with latex condoms, spermicides are especially effective.

- **Most non-barrier birth control methods do not prevent the spread of STDS.** Norplant, Depoprovera and birth control pills *do not provide any protection against STDs.* Spermicide, diaphragms and cervical caps give some protection. Latex condoms used correctly every time give the best protection, but even they are not 100% effective.

- **Don't be shy or embarrassed.** It is always better to be assertive, to take precautions and insist on safe sex. Protecting your health is your responsibility. Be aware, too, that alcohol hinders your ability to make sound decisions. Remember, some STDs are incurable, and HIV can cause death. That's too high a price to pay for simply feeling embarrassed.

# Part Five

## _Other Concerns_

# CHAPTER 25

## *Breastfeeding*

### Breastfeeding and Birth Control

The birth control needs of a woman change after the birth of a baby. If she has completed her family, she'll need a long-term contraceptive to prevent future pregnancies. If she has not completed her family, she'll need a reversible form of birth control that will allow her to appropriately space her children. Appropriate spacing is important, because, according to research, a baby born within fifteen months of the last child has a 33% greater chance of prematurity. If the mother is breastfeeding, she'll need to use a contraceptive that is not only reliable but also safe for the breastfed baby.

### Lactational Amenorrhea Method

The absence of period during breastfeeding is known as

lactational amenorrhea. Using breast-feeding as the sole method of birth control is known as the lactational amenorrhea method (LAM). Researchers have found that the sucking stimulus of breastfeeding inhibits the production of the hormone that causes the ovary to release the egg. When LAM is used properly, failure rate is about 2%.

The cardinal rules about using LAM are:

- The time period between nursing the baby or using a breast pump to extract the milk should not exceed four hours.

- There should be no vaginal bleeding past the first few weeks after childbirth. If bleeding persists or resumes after four weeks, another contraceptive method should be used. LAM should not be used for more than six months.

## Birth Control Pills

Combination birth control pills, which contain estrogen, decrease the amount of breast milk. The estrogen also passes into the breast milk. As a result, doctors usually avoid prescribing combination birth control pills for the first six months after childbirth, if the mother is breast-feeding. Progestin-only pills (which contain proges-terone), also known as the mini-pills, can be started six weeks after childbirth.

## Tubal Ligation

When a woman is absolutely sure that she has completed her family, she may decide to have tubal ligation, one of the most common methods of birth control used in the United States. About 28% of women use tubal ligation to prevent pregnancy. Tubal ligation can sometimes be done immediately after childbirth, which saves the woman from a second hospital stay. It can be done under local or general anesthesia. In this procedure, a small incision is made below the belly button. The fallopian tubes can be easily accessed through this incision. The tubes are cut and tied and a portion of them is removed.

## Diaphragm

Women should be fitted for the diaphragm no sooner than six weeks after childbirth. If she used a diaphragm prior to her pregnancy, she must be re-fitted, because childbirth can alter the size of the vagina. Some form of spermicide should be used with the diaphragm.

## Intrauterine Devices

For women who want a long-term contraception an IUD is an excellent choice. IUDs are usually inserted six weeks after the birth of a baby. This is a reversible method of contraception and when used for several consecutive years, is less costly than other birth control methods.

## Depoprovera and Norplants

They can be started six weeks after childbirth. They have not been found to decrease milk production or have any harmful effects on breastfed babies. Some women prefer these methods, because they are long-acting.

## Condoms and Spermicides

Condoms and spermicides can be used safely during breastfeeding. Spermicides can also help relieve vaginal dryness, which is common after childbirth.

## Fertility Awareness Methods

These include the rhythm method, the basal body temperature method and the cervical mucus method. These methods are unreliable for the first few months after childbirth.

Many couples use condoms, diaphragms, or spermicides to complement the natural birth control effect of breast-feeding. These options have the least effect on breastfed babies, and they give couples a few months to decide on a longer-term contraception.

# References

American Medical Association Harris Poll. 1995. Available online at www.arhp.org./hs/fall96/wayne.htm.

Klein L, Stewart F. "Preconception Care." Hatcher, et al. *Contraception Technology.* 17th Revised Edition, (New York); 1998:623-633.

Davis A, Godwin A, Lippman J, et al. "Triphasic norgestimate-ethinyl estradiol for treating dysfunctional uterine bleeding." *Obstetrics and Gynecology.* 2000; 96:913-920

Grimes DA, Godwin AJ, Rubin A, et al. "Ovulation and follicular development associated with three low dose oral contraceptives: a randomized controlled trial." *Obstetrics and Gynecology.* 1994; 83(1): 29-34

"Maternal mortality–United States, 1982-1996." MMWR *Morbidity and Mortality Weekly Report.* 1998; 47(34):705-707.

Teichmann AT, Brill K, Albring M, et al. "The influence of the dose of ethinylestradiol in oral contraceptives on follicle growth." *Gynecologic Endocrinology.* 1995; 9:299-305

Casper RF, Dodin S, Reid Rl, et al. "The effect of 20 ug ethinyl estradio/1mg norethindrone acetate (Minestrin), a low-dose oral contraceptive, on vaginal bleeding patterns, hot flashes, and quality of life in symptomatic peri-menopausal women." *Menopause.* 1997; 4:139-147

Mishra GD, Dobson AJ, Schofield MJ. "Cigarette smoking, menstrual symptoms and miscarriage among young women." *Aust NZ Journal of Public Health.* 2000; 24(4):413-420.

Henshaw SK. "Unintended pregnancy in the United States." *Family Planning Perspective.* 1998; 30 (1):24-29, 46.

Solheim F. "An assessment of quality of life in women treated with Depoprovera in Sweden." In: Zambrano D, ed. Depoprovera (medroxyprogesterone acetate) for contraception. A current perspective of scientific, clinical and social issues. Proceedings of an international symposium held on 19-20 November 1992. Oxford: Oxford Clinical Communications, 1992:61-72

Cancer and Steroid Hormone Study of the Centers for Disease Control and the National Institute of Child Health and Human Development. "Combination oral contraceptive use and the risk of endometrial cancer." *Journal of American Medical Association.* 1987; 257:796-800

Landis SH, Murray T, Bolden S, et al. *Cancer statistics, 1998.* CA Cancer J Clin. 1998; 48:6-29

Lucky AW, Henderson TA, Olson WH, et al. "The effectiveness of norgestimate and ethinyl estradiol in treating moderate acne vulgaris." *Journal of American Academy of Dermatology.* 1997; 37(5 Pt1): 746-754

Chez R, Rowlands S. "Emergency postcoital contraception." *Contemporary Ob/Gyn* 1994; 39:78-88

Centers for Disease Control and Prevention. "Division of STD/HIV" *Prevention 1992 Annual Report.* Atlanta, Georgia: CDC, 1993

Jones EF, Forrest JD. "Contraceptive failure rates based on the 1988 National Survey of Family Growth." *Family Planning Perspective* 1992, 24:12-19

Redmond GP, Olson WH, Lippman JS, et al. "A randomized, placebo-controlled trial of norgestimate and ethinyl estradiol in the treatment of acne vulgaris." *Obstetrics and Gynecology.* 1997; 89 (4): 615-522

Morse BA, Hutchins E. "Reducing complications from alcohol use during pregnancy through screening." *Journal of American Medical Womens Association.* 2000; 55(4):225-227,240.

Trussell J, Warner DL, Hatcher RA. "Condom slippage and breakage rates." *Family Planning Perspective* 1992; 24:20-23

Mathews TJ, Curtin SC, MacDorman MF. "Infant mortality statistics from the 1998 period linked birth/infant death data set." *National Vital Statistics Report.* 2000; 48(12):1-25.

Webster LA, Berman SM, Greenspan JR. "Surveillance for gonorrhea and primary and secondary syphilis among adolescents, United States—1981-1991." *Morbidity and Mortality Weekly Report* 1993; 42 (SS-3):1-11

Wiseman A, Bowie J, Cogswell D, Dewsbury J, Hamilton M, Hutchinson F, et al. Marvelon; "Clinical experience in the UK." *British Journal of Family Planning* 1984; 10 (9): 38-42

Goldzieher JW, Moses LE, Averkin E, Scheel C, Taber BZ. "A placebo-controlled double-blind crossover investigation of the side effects attributed to oral contraceptives." *Fertility Sterility* 1971; 22:609-623

Oakley GP, Erickson JD, James LM, et al. "Prevention of folic acid-preventable spina bifida and anencephaly." *Ciba Foundation Symposium.* 1994; 181(4):212-222.

Jones WK. *Safe Motherhood At-A-Glance 2000:* "Preventing pregnancy-related illness and death."

Harlap S. Oral Contraceptives and breast cancer. "Cause and effect?" *Journal of Reproductive Medicine* 1991; 36:374-395

Rosenberg M. "Weight change with oral contraceptive use and during the menstrual cycle." *Contraception.* 1998; 58:345-349

Gallup Organization. "Attitudes Toward Contraceptives Survey conducted for the American College of Obstetrics and Gynecology." Princeton, NJ 1985

Shoupe D, Mishell DR Jr, Bopp BL, Fielding M. "The significance of bleeding patterns in Norplant implant users." *Obstetrics and Gynecology* 1991; 77:256-260

Henshaw SK. "Teenage abortion, birth and pregnancy statistics by state, 1988." *Family Planning Perspective* 1993; 25:122-126

Redmond GP, Olson WH, Lippman JS, Kafrissen ME, Jones TM, Jorizzo JL. "Norgestimate and ethinyl estradiol in the treatment of acne vulgaris: a randomized, placebo-controlled trial." *Obstetrics and Gynecology* 1997; 89:615-622

Milsom I, Sundell G, Andersch B. "The influence of different combined oral contraceptives on the prevalence and severity of dysmenorrhea." *Contraception.* 1990; 42:497-506

Ortho-McNeil Pharmaceutical Corporation, Inc. "1998 Annual Birth Control Study." Ortho-McNeil Pharmaceutical Corporation, Inc. Raritan, NJ 1998

Collaborative Group on Hormonal Factors in Breast Cancer. "Breast cancer and hormonal contraceptives: collaborative reanalysis of individual data on 53,297 women with breast cancer and 100,239 women without breast cancer from 54 epidemiological studies." Lancet. 1996; 347:1713-1727

Lippman JS, Godwin A, Olson W. "The tolerability of a triphasic norgestimate/EE containing OC: results from a double-blind, placebo-controlled trial." *Primary Care Update Ob/Gyn* 1998; 5:173-174

"State-specific maternal mortality among black and white women–United States, 1987-1996." *MMWR Morbidity and Mortality Weekly Report.* 1999; 48(23):492-496

Rohan TE, Miller AB. "A cohort study of oral contraceptive use and risk of benign breast disease." *International Journal of Cancer.* 1999; 82(2): 191-196

Yuzpe AA, Smith RP, Rademaker AW. "A multicenter clinical investigation employing ethinyl estradiol combined with dl-norgestrel as a postcoital contraceptive agent." *Fertility and Sterility* 1982; 37:508-513

Lee NC, Rubin GL, Borucki R. "The intrauterine device and pelvic inflammatory disease revisited: new results from the Women's Health Study". *Obstetrics and Gynecology* 1988; 72:1-6

Yuzpe AA, Lancee WJ. "Ethinylestradiol and dl-norgestrel as a posticoital contraceptive." *Fertility and Sterility* 1977; 28:932-936

Charreau I Plu-Bureau G, Bachelot A, et al. "Oral contraceptive use and risk of benign breast disease in a French case-control study of young women." *European Journal of Cancer Prevention.* 1993; 2:147-154

Schlesselman JJ. "Net effect of oral contraceptive use on the risk of cancer in women in the United States." *Obstetrics and Gynecology.* 1995; 85:793-801

Larsson G, Milsom I, Lindstedt G, Rybo G. "The influence of a low-dose combined oral contraceptive on menstrual blood loss and iron status." *Contraception.* 1992; 46:327-334

Kessel E. "Pelvic inflammatory disease with intrauterine device use: a reassessment." *Fertility and Sterility* 1989; 51:1-11

Abma J. Chandra A, Mosher W, et al. "Fertility, family planning, and women's health: New data from the 1995 National Survey of Family Growth." National Center for Health Statistics. *Vital Health Statistics.* 1997;23(19).

Trussell J, Ellertson C. "The efficacy of emergency contraception." *Fertility Control Review* 1995; 4:8-11

Webb A. "How safe is the Yuzpe method of emergency contraception?" *Fertility Control Review* 1995; 4:16-18

Wilcox AJ, Weinberg CR, Baird DD. "Timing of sexual intercourse in relation to ovulation. Effects on the probability of conception, survival of the pregnancy, and sex of the baby." *New England Journal of Medicine* 1995; 333:1517-1521

Hillard PJA. "The patient's reaction to side effects of oral contraception." *American Journal of Obstetrics and Gynecology.* 1989; 161:1412-1415

"LAM 98% Effective, If Certain Rules are Followed." *Contraception Technology* Update 17, nos 1. (January 1996):6

"Contraceptive Ring Gets FDA approval" *Ob. Gyn.News* November 1, 2001;1,4

Audet MC, Moreau M, Koltun WD, et al, for the Ortho Evra/Evra 004 Study Group. "Evaluation of contraceptive efficacy and cycle control of a transdermal contraceptive patch vs an oral contraceptive: a randomized controlled trail." *Journal of the American Medical Association.* 2001;258:2347-2354.

Zieman M. Guillebaud E, Weisberg G, et al. "Integrated summary of contraceptive efficacy with the Ortho Evra/Evra transdermal system." *Fertility and Sterility.* 2001; 76(3 suppl 1):S19. Abstract.

# Index

# Quick Order Form

**Fax orders:** 973-779-1689 (Send this form.)

**Telephone orders: Toll Free 877-959-1900**

**Email orders:** orders@birthcontroladvice.com

**Postal Orders:** Nipari Publishing, Ramapo Valley Road, PO Box 230, Oakland, NJ 07436

**Please send more FREE information on:**

☐ Special Reports       ☐ Speaking/Seminars

☐ Mailing Lists       ☐ Consulting

Name:_____

Address: _____

City:_____State_____ZIP: _____

Telephone: _____

Email address: _____

**Sales tax:** Please add 6% for products shipped to New Jersey addresses.

**Shipping & Handling — US:** $4.00   **International:** $9.00

Payment: ☐ Check   ☐ Credit card: _____

      ☐ Visa     ☐ MasterCard     ☐ AMEX     ☐ Discover

Card Number: _____

Name on card (Please print): _____

Signature: _____

For latest information visit: www.birthcontroladvice.com